As one of the world's longest established
and best-known travel brands,
Thomas Cook are the experts in travel.

For more than 135 years our
guidebooks have unlocked the secrets
of destinations around the world,
sharing with travellers a wealth of
experience and a passion for travel.

**Rely on Thomas Cook as your
travelling companion on your next trip
and benefit from our unique heritage.**

Thomas Cook **pocket** guides

AARHUS

Thomas
Cook

Your travelling companion since 1873

Written by Nicol Foulkes, updated by Marc Di Duca

Published by Thomas Cook Publishing
A division of Thomas Cook Tour Operations Limited
Company registration no. 3772199 England
The Thomas Cook Business Park, Unit 9, Coningsby Road,
Peterborough PE3 8SB, United Kingdom
Email: books@thomascook.com, Tel: +44 (0) 1733 416477
www.thomascookpublishing.com

Produced by Cambridge Publishing Management Limited
Burr Elm Court, Main Street, Caldecote CB23 7NU
www.cambridgepm.co.uk

ISBN: 978-1-84848-430-6

First edition © 2008 Thomas Cook Publishing
This second edition © 2011
Text © Thomas Cook Publishing
Maps © Thomas Cook Publishing/PCGraphics (UK) Limited
Transport map © Communicarta Limited

Series Editor: Karen Beaulah
Production/DTP: Steven Collins

Printed and bound in Spain by GraphyCems

Cover photography © Stephen Roberts Photography/Alamy

CONTENTS

SYMBOLS KEY

The following symbols are used throughout this book:

ⓐ address **ⓣ** telephone **ⓦ** website address **ⓔ** email
ⓛ opening times **ⓝ** public transport connections **ⓘ** important

The following symbols are used on the maps:

ⓘ	information office	▓	point of interest
✈	airport	○	city
✚	hospital	○	large town
🛡	police station	○	small town
▣	bus station	▭	motorway
▤	railway station	—	main road
✝	cathedral	—	minor road
❶	numbers denote featured cafés & restaurants	—	railway

Hotels and restaurants are graded by approximate price as follows:
£ budget price   **££** mid-range price   **£££** expensive

▶ *Aarhus's cathedral tower and spire*

INTRODUCING

Aarhus

Introduction

Aarhus, often referred to in Denmark as 'the City of Smiles', has a particularly open, friendly and positive vibe.

This is partially explained by the city's large student population: there are over 25 different academic institutions here (including a university), and, in fact, every fifth resident is engaged in some kind of academic pursuit. Their presence has created the sociological phenomenon with which, in typical Danish style, the city is identified – *den kreative grobund* (the breeding ground for creativity).

Way beyond the academic world, Aarhus attracts people who are generally open to life's possibilities, who want to initiate projects and actively engage with the city and its inhabitants.

All these factors taken together provide Aarhus's infectious energy and explain why it is so alive with cultural projects. For, in addition to the keen penchant for design and modern, urban development that you find all over Denmark, Aarhus distinguishes itself by nurturing a cultural scene that attracts and inspires locals and visitors alike.

Radiating out westwards from Denmark's largest shipping port, Aarhus is in the Jutland region. The city has youth – it's the country's youngest city – and good looks. It also has ambition: planners are transforming the harbour area and extending it northwards, in order to make room for new residents as well as to cater for the increasing numbers of tourists. A period of rapid, ambitious growth is under way and it includes such exciting ventures as the 20-year plan to create a *Sports Ramblas* – a boulevard exclusively dedicated to sporting activities.

◆ *Cycling through the colourful city streets*

Other cities may be better known, but mere familiarity is in itself no recommendation; Aarhus has no laurels on which to rest, no tired old clichés to call upon and no received image to live up to. Few can match the city for beauty, friendliness and fun. Word's getting around, and pretty soon everyone will want a piece of the action. No wonder Aarhus has a smile on its face.

When to go

The combination of the weather and the natural beauty of the city make summer the best time to visit. However, if you want to take advantage of the great cultural scene, come between May and October. During the Christmas period the city becomes particularly festive, with beautiful street decorations, markets in the Ridehuset and Den Gamle By and the smell of *gløgg* (mulled wine) wafting from the cafés in Vadestedet and the Latin Kvarteret (Latin Quarter).

SEASONS & CLIMATE

Aarhus's winters are considerably colder than the UK's, with the wind chill making it feel even nippier. The average temperature in January and February tends to hover just above freezing. The April-to-September temperature range is between 13 and 28°C (55–82°F), and can fluctuate between the two within 24 hours. Between mid-September and November, expect a reasonable amount of sunshine, but with some rain and temperatures anywhere between 5 and 15°C (41–59°F).

ANNUAL EVENTS

The city's gloriously rich cultural life is reflected in the number of different festivals and events that happen from May onwards. In addition to the most unique and popular event of the year, the Århus Festuge (Aarhus Festival, see page 14), there's a plethora of enticements at which this guide has room only to hint. Each year brings something new, so check what's on with the tourist office (see page 135) when you plan your visit.

◯ *An installation by Angie Hiesl at Århus Festuge*

May

Colliers Classic Cykelløb (Colliers Classic Bike Race) Teams from around the world saddle up and push off at the start of the month. For further information contact the tourist office.
ⓐ Banegårdspladsen 20 ❶ 87 31 50 10 Ⓦ www.visitaarhus.com
Vikingebymarked (Viking Town Market) Take this opportunity to experience what it was like to shop at a Viking market.
ⓐ Store Torv, Bispetorv ❶ 87 31 50 10 Ⓦ www.visitaarhus.com
Ⓝ Bus: 3, 7, 14 to Skolebakken; train to Skolebakken

June & July

SPOT Festival The Musikhuset and Ridehuset become chock-a-block with Nordic rock.  86 12 84 44 www.spotfestival.dk Bus: 3, 4, 14, 16, 17, 18, 25 to Ridehuset

Århus Middelaldermarked (Aarhus Middle Ages Festival) Midsummer (21 June) marks the start of a three-day re-creation of medieval life. Vennelyst Parken, Nørreport 50 51 92 65

Festival week in Den Gamle By has something for everyone

Ⓦ www.aamm.dk Ⓛ Check website Ⓝ Bus: 14, 56, 58 to
Århus Sygehus

Sankt Hans Aften (Saint John's Eve) The evening of 23 June
sees Århusianers, along with the rest of the country, lighting
bonfires to celebrate midsummer.

Danmarks største chill-out (Denmark's biggest chill-out)
Grab a picnic and join the locals in the park for a late July
relaxathon, with DJs supplying trippy chill-out music.
Ⓐ Vennelyst Parken Ⓦ www.stella-polaris.dk
Ⓝ Bus: 14, 56, 58 to Århus Sygehus

August & September
Sommerballet (Summer Ballet) Bring along a hamper to the
Concert Hall lawn for ballet at the beginning of the month.
Ⓐ Thomas Jensens Allé Ⓣ 89 40 40 40 Ⓦ www.musikhusetaarhus.dk
Ⓝ Bus: 3, 4, 14, 16, 17, 18, 25 to Ridehuset
Pop Revo A three-day pop festival held in Pakhuset, a beautiful
warehouse by the docks (see page 75). Ⓐ Nordhavnsgade 1
Ⓣ 40 90 40 64 Ⓦ www.studenterhusaarhus.dk
Ⓝ Bus: 91 to Pakhuset

October
Mad-marked (Organic Food Market) This three-day event
allows you to experience Danish cuisine guilt-, pesticide-
and additive-free. Ⓐ Check website for location Ⓣ 22 33 14 94
Ⓦ www.organic.dk
Kulturnatten (Culture Night) A mid-month celebration of Aarhus's
cultural scene. Ⓐ (Secretariat) Nordhavnsgade 1 Ⓣ 51 71 79 02
Ⓦ www.kulturnataarhus.dk

November & December
Juleparade (Christmas Parade) On 30 November Santa leads the Christmas Parade through the city centre, officially declaring Aarhus open for festivities.
Jul i Den Gamle By (Christmas in the Old Town) Christmas celebrations rage through December and end on New Year's Eve in the famous Den Gamle By Old Town (see page 62). ⓐ Viborgvej 2 ⓘ 86 12 31 88 ⓦ www.dengamleby.dk ⓝ Bus: 3, 14, 25 to Den Gamle By

PUBLIC HOLIDAYS
Nytårs dag (New Year's Day) 1 January
Skærtorsdag (Maundy Thursday) 5 April 2012; 28 March 2013
Langfredag (Good Friday) 6 April 2012; 29 March 2013
2 Påskedag (Easter Monday) 9 April 2012; 1 April 2013
Stor Bededag (Common Prayer Day) Fourth Friday after Good Friday
Kristi himmelfartsdag (Ascension Day) 17 May 2012; 9 May 2013
2 Pinsedag (Whit Monday) 28 May 2012; 20 May 2013
Grundlovsdag (Constitution Day) 5 June
Juleferie (Christmas) 24–6 December

Banks, post offices, public buildings and most shops close on public holidays and public transport runs to Sunday schedules.

Århus Festuge

Århus Festuge (Aarhus Festival) has been taking place annually since 1965. Now recognised as one of northern Europe's most diverse cultural festivals, it encompasses hundreds of events and activities over ten days of dance, music, exhibitions, theatre, opera, kids' culture, sport and entertainment.

Unlike most other city festivals, Aarhus's pursues a specific theme each year. For example, 2010's was Naboer (neighbours) and others have included Hans Christian Andersen (2005), Womania (2006) and Open City (2008). The fact that performances and events have to be relevant to a given theme keeps the festival fresh and vital. Events always stir up debate across the city and this being Scandinavia, things always run a bit deeper than one might expect. In 2007 the theme was In Motion, which prompted debates about the future of the city and the world, the nature of time and – the big one – the movement of traffic through the city. Deep stuff indeed.

Over the decades the Århus Festuge has attracted thousands of local artists, as well as some surprisingly big names. The dance troupe Stomp, The Rolling Stones, Ravi Shankar, the London Royal Philharmonic Orchestra, Nigel Kennedy, Björk, Rage Against the Machine and Green Day have all made appearances.

Whatever the theme is, the whole of the city gets involved, and its parks, restaurants, theatres and museums all become specialist venues. The main aim is to have fun and discover the city's diverse and ever-evolving cultural scene, so if you're in town, you really shouldn't miss it. Actually, you won't be able to. ⓐ Administration: Officersbygningen, Vester Allé 3 ⓣ 89 40 91 91 ⓦ www.aarhusfestuge.dk

🔺 Show spectacle, the Lions of Senegal, visit the Århus Festuge

History

The name Aarhus originates from the Middle Ages, but the location is referred to in Icelandic chronicles as 'Árós', meaning 'River Mouth' or 'River Delta'. The city's first real impression on recorded history dates from the 9th century, when Jutland became the Vikings' headquarters. The trail then goes somewhat cold until the 1620s, when the Germans advanced upon Aarhus (you can still see some of their forts located to the south of the city). This incursion seems to have awoken various neighbouring countries to the good news that is Aarhus, and in the 1640s and 1650s the Swedes attacked and occupied the city on several occasions.

Both the Swedes and the Germans had realised that Aarhus is located in a geographically favourable position: it is at the heart of Denmark on the mainland peninsula of Jutland, which allowed successful trading with the German states, the Baltic countries, Norway, Holland, France and England.

In the early 19th century, the city really began to flourish and distinguish itself from the other major ports in nearby Copenhagen and Hamburg. The 20th century saw the city blossom, and its late development can be attributed to the Danish Industrial Revolution of that period, when thousands of people moved from the countryside to the cities to find work. With the expansion of the rail network and harbour, the population increased to a great extent; by 1920, it surpassed that of nearby Aalborg, making it Jutland's largest, and Denmark's second-largest, city. Its most challenging period of the 20th century – and perhaps of all time – came between

1940 and 1945, when, like the rest of Denmark, it was occupied by the Germans. Danish cooperation with Germany nevertheless continued – at least economically – until 1943, when, in an act of protest, the Danish navy sank most of its ships and sent its officers north, to neutral Sweden.

Nowadays, the Inner City is home to just over 300,000 people. Plans are already laid for the expansion of the city to house a further 100,000 citizens before 2030. The University of Aarhus is progressing rapidly, with its academic record gaining increasing international recognition each year. The university, together with all the city's other educational establishments, places Aarhus way above the national average for educational attainment and contributes enormously to the city today.

Another source of valuable cultural diversity is the 12 per cent of Aarhus's population that come from other shores. This unusually high number of immigrants (the national average is around 6 per cent) is made up of Lebanese, Turks, Somalis, Iraqis, Iranians, Vietnamese, Poles, Germans, Norwegians and Brits. Unlike, say, in Copenhagen, many of the larger migrant groups live on the outskirts of the city, which is just beginning to cause some tension as 'ghettos' are formed.

The city is currently undergoing a major transformation, with the harbour area being extended northwards to create a separate social and living space, and various projects being undertaken to improve the integration of foreign nationals and immigrants. This is Denmark's greatest challenge at present; one gets the feeling that Aarhus's open and welcoming nature will see it through.

Lifestyle

In terms of lifestyle, the most influential word in the Danish language is *hygge* (pronounced 'who-ga'). A translation? That's a tough one – you'll only really get it when you've been here a while. But for now think of cosy, atmospheric, enjoyable and intimate combined and you won't be far off. 'Charismatic' might sum it up. However you translate it, the City of Smiles has *hygge* nailed. This is a buzzing yet laid-back place where the inhabitants operate at a distinct beat below the tempo of Europe's bigger cities. Perhaps most importantly from a visitor's point of view, Aarhus is quintessentially friendly.

Danes are spending more and more time socialising outside their homes: these days, workers frequently meet in bars after work for a quick drink before heading home (Århusianers are making an admirable stand against the trend for living life as corporate wage-slaves); students grab a six-pack and sit by the harbour, river or in one of the city's gardens. A definite café culture is beginning to develop. However, it is still very much the thing for locals to have a nice meal at home with friends over a good bottle of red wine and then head out into town. The manifold pleasures of social intercourse are of paramount importance here.

Take a leisurely stroll along the coastline beach

Culture

Aarhus is provincial (not always a pejorative term) in the sense that it really has only one centre (as paradoxical as it may sound; cities often have several). But at the same time it has everything a big city has: cinemas and galleries, a mighty big art museum, cafés and clubs, great shopping opportunities and enough space for every expression of its inhabitants' personalities: there's a tango culture, a salsa culture, a street/punk/underground scene and a thriving gay scene.

Of course, it's not all unbridled hedonism: Aarhus has its spiritual side, with plenty of churches scattered around the city. The official state religion is the Evangelical Lutheran Church of Denmark, but there are also a significant number of Catholics and a growing number of Muslims. However, while most Danes belong to a church, very few actually practise religion and the country has a high number of atheists and agnostics. The Church plays a cultural rather than a religious role in people's lives, as can be seen at Christmas time, baptisms, confirmations, weddings and funerals.

Aarhus also resonates to a distinctly academic vibe. The university has been growing constantly since 1928, making this a city of creative minds. Whereas its cultural life used to revolve around the academic institutes, recent cooperation between them, the city council and industry has been hugely successful: the cultural scene in Aarhus has exploded. The last quarter of a century has seen the advent of Musikhuset (the Concert Hall, see page 71), which plays host to the Aarhus Symphony Orchestra; Den Jyske Opera (Jutland's Opera); **Det Jyske Musikkonservatorium**

🔺 *The Aarhus Symphony Orchestra performs in the Musikhuset*

(**Jutland's Music Academy** ⓐ Skovgaardsgade 2C ⓣ 72 26 74 00
ⓦ www.musikkons.dk); the Børneteatret Filuren (children's
theatre group); the Stenomuseet (the Steno Museum, see page
84); and the ARoS Århus Kunstmuseum (Aarhus Art Museum),
one of the largest museums in northern Europe (see page 66).

Aarhus is famed in Denmark for nurturing musical talent,
and the range of music festivals (see Annual events, page 8)
is evidence of its significance. Art also plays a great role. As well
as the larger galleries and art museums, be sure to visit some of
the smaller galleries and shops where you'll have the opportunity
to meet the artists themselves. Check out in particular:

Galleri Jarsbo ⓐ Store Torv 6, 4 ⓣ 86 21 12 86 ⓦ http://jarsbo.dk
ⓛ 12.00–17.00 Mon–Wed & Fri, 11.00–14.00 Sat & Sun, closed
Thur
Gallerie MøllerWitt ⓐ Vestergade 56A ⓣ 86 18 29 49
ⓦ www.gmw.dk ⓛ 11.30–17.00 Tues–Fri, 10.00–15.00 Sat,
closed Sun & Mon
Ulrik Witts Hus ⓐ Volden 23 ⓣ 23 46 45 08 ⓦ www.kunstruten.dk
ⓛ 12.00–17.30 Tues–Thur, 12.00–19.00 Fri, 10.00–14.00 Sat,
closed Sun & Mon

The inhabitants of the city are encouraged to get involved
in developing Aarhus's cultural scene. Strong Bright Hearts
(ⓦ www.strongbrighthearts.com) is an Internet community, the
members of which have started up projects like 'Share Your
Heart' (ⓦ www.shareyourheart.com), an initiative encouraging
people to express optimism for the future. This unique approach
to development ties in with the general focus of the city
towards openness, inclusiveness and creativity.

▶ *Summer in the city*

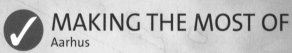

MAKING THE MOST OF
Aarhus

Shopping

Aarhus is made up of three main districts, Midtby (the Inner City), Trøjborg and Frederiksbjerg. Trøjborg's reputation of having rather prosaic purchasing possibilities means that tourists generally prefer the Inner City and Frederiksbjerg for shopping.

The major shopping muscles can be most pleasurably flexed in the Inner City. Three of its pedestrianised streets are known collectively as **Strøget**, and here you'll find Georg Jensen (see opposite), Denmark's most famous jewellery designer, fashion stores and all the usual high-street shops. The cathedral area is also littered with shopping opportunities, including **Bang & Olufsen** (ⓐ Klostergade 14 ⓣ 86 12 29 22 ⓦ www.bang-olufsen.com). The Latin Quarter has numerous funky designer shops. For truly unique finds, hit the smaller, independent shops of Mejlgade, Klostergade, Badstuegade, Guldsmedgade and Volden.

The central station at the bottom of Strøget and the train lines mark the boundary to Frederiksbjerg with the dinky **Bruuns Galleri** shopping centre (ⓐ M P Bruuns Gade 25 ⓣ 70 20 89 09 ⓦ www.bruunsgalleri.dk). Here are many international chain stores such as **H&M** (ⓐ Falkoner Allé ⓣ 36 97 80 40 ⓦ www.hm.com), alongside sportswear shops, gift shops and the multiplex Cinemaxx (see page 33). M P Bruuns Gade is distinguished by a marvellous cheese shop, some lovely kids' boutiques and knick-knack shops. Wander down Jægergårdsgade to find all sorts of items for the home.

AND THE TOP THREE GIFT SHOPS ARE ...

Georg Jensen Just the job for designer silverware. ⓐ Søndergade 1
ⓣ 86 12 01 00 ⓦ www.georgjensen.dk ⓛ 10.00–17.00 Mon–Thur,
10.00–19.00 Fri, 10.00–16.00 Sat, closed Sun

Hay A specialist in Danish design furniture and soft home
furnishings and winner of the Danish Designer Prize 2007.
ⓐ Rosenkrantzgade 24 ⓣ 99 42 44 20 ⓦ www.hay.dk
ⓛ 10.00–17.30 Mon–Thur, 10.00–18.00 Fri, 10.00–15.00 Sat,
closed Sun

LYNfabrikken The place to go for Århusian, contemporary
designer gifts: lampshades, ceramics, jewellery, stationery and
apparel. ⓐ Vestergade 49B ⓣ 87 30 00 75 ⓦ www.lynfabrikken.dk
ⓛ 10.00–18.00 Mon–Sat, closed Sun

USEFUL SHOPPING PHRASES

What time does the shop open/close?
Hvornår åbner/lukker butikken?
Vohnor orbna/lorka boo-teeken?

How much is this? I'd like to buy it.
Hvor meget koster det? Jeg vil gerne købe det.
Vohr mah-eht kosta di? Yai vi gairneh ker-be di.

This is too large/too small. Do you have any others?
Den er for stor/lille. Har du andre?
Dehn air fo store/lilla. Hah doo andera?

Eating & drinking

Aarhus's location – right by the sea, in the heart of an agricultural region – allows its restaurateurs to work with the finest produce that Denmark has to offer. Traditional eateries offering roast pork and potatoes, steak and some fish dishes are easy to find (Aarhus has Scandinavia's best fishmongers), as are more modern restaurants offering organic and vegetarian options. The city's large immigrant population is reflected in the wide range of cuisines here. As well as Italian, you'll find, among others, Argentinean, Greek, Turkish, Chinese, Thai and Spanish restaurants.

The Danes are a nation of wine lovers. Most of the cafés and restaurants offer a good selection of fine wines, many with organic options, but do be aware that the cost of the wine makes a big difference to your bill. Beers have also seen a revival over the past few years, with a huge increase in the numbers of reputable local breweries in the Greater Aarhus area and a broader selection of foreign and organic ales than ever before. Aarhus has its own signature beer, 'Århus sættet'.

Most cafés open between 09.00 and 10.00. Restaurants usually start serving evening meals around 17.00, and the kitchens

PRICE CATEGORIES
Based on the average price per head for a three-course dinner, excluding drinks. Lunch will usually be a little cheaper in each category.
£ under 200kr **££** 200–350kr **£££** over 350kr

in both cafés and restaurants usually close at about 22.00. It is not customary to tip; however, it is nice to do so if you have had a pleasant experience.

The favourite everyday snack here is *smørrebrød*, a traditional type of open sandwich consisting of a slice of dark rye bread with a topping. It is small enough to be a no-cutlery-required nibble if you're on the move or having a picnic.

● *Riverside cafés fill up in the Vadestedet area of the city*

PICNIC BASKET

There are several good delis, bakeries and supermarkets around if you want to create your own picnic basket or if you are self-catering.

Byens Ost A wonderful deli selling cheese, cured meats, snacks, seasoned oils, wines and more. ⓐ M P Bruuns Gade 54 ⓣ 86 12 24 74 ⓛ 10.00–17.30 Mon–Thur, 10.00–18.30 Fri, 10.00–13.30 Sat, closed Sun

Emmerys An Århusian bakery and small café which now has branches all over Denmark. ⓐ Guldsmedgade 24–26/M P Bruuns Gade 49 ⓣ 87 30 06 40 ⓦ www.emmerys.dk ⓛ 07.00–18.00 Mon–Thur, 07.00–19.00 Fri, 07.00–16.00 Sat, 07.00–15.00 Sun

Gårdbutikken A small organic supermarket near the harbour. ⓐ Kystvejen 5 ⓣ 86 93 02 44 ⓦ www.gaardbutikken.dk ⓛ 10.00–18.00 Mon–Fri, 09.00–14.00 Sat, closed Sun

▲ *Emmerys has everything you need for your picnic in Aarhus*

USEFUL DINING PHRASES

I would like a table for ...
Jeg vil gerne købe et bord til ...
Yai vi gairneh ker-be at board til ...

I am a vegetarian
Jeg er vegetar
Yai air veggehtar

Where is the toilet (restroom), please?
Hvor er toilettet, tak?
Vohr air toylehdeht, tahg?

May I have the bill, please?
Jeg vil gerne betale regningen?
Yai vi gairneh bitaileh rhiningehn?

Do you accept credit cards?
Tager i kreditkort?
Tah ee krehdeetkort?

Jeremys Bakery How many bakeries in Denmark are run by an English guy called – you guessed it – Jeremy? This one sells great bread sandwiches and muffins. ⓐ Mejlgade 17 ⓣ 86 76 19 13 ⓦ www.jeremys.dk ⓛ 07.30–18.00 Mon–Fri, 07.30–15.00 Sat, closed Sun

Entertainment & nightlife

The nightlife in the city is mainly centred around the Århus Å (Aarhus River); the area along Åboulevarden, known as **Vadestedet**, is the real focus of fun. Despite the number of students in the city, Aarhus does not really have a trendy club scene. The nightclubs that exist are actually discos, and men and women searching for that special soulmate are somewhat overrepresented. Still, if you fancy a bit of a dance among these strutting peacocks, try **La Belle Night Club** (ⓐ Mindegade 6 ⓦ www.labelle.dk) or **Social Club** (ⓐ Klostergade 34 ⓦ www.socialclub.dk).

Perhaps a more enjoyable (and certainly more Århusian) way to spend an evening is in one of the city's café-bars or even

a *værtshus* or *bodega* (the Danes' version of a pub). There's no shortage of café options and seriously inebriated locals along Vadestedet; the Latin Quarter is slightly more peaceful, though. Don't miss the Teater Bodega (see page 74) by the cathedral and theatre, even if you just pop in to look at the amazing illustrated history of Aarhus's nightlife.

Another option is to go and listen to some live music. The venues are scattered around the city, but are all within walking distance of one another. Try one of the following: **Fatter Eskil** (ⓐ Skolegade 25 ⓦ www.fattereskil.dk) or the Irish pub **Tir na nóg** (ⓐ Frederiksgade 40 ⓦ www.tirnanog.dk). Other concert venues include **Turbinehallen** (ⓐ Kalkværksvej 12

● *Enjoy the riverside ambience at dusk in one of the many outdoor restaurants*

PUBS & *VÆRTSHUSER*

Aarhus is an old harbour town, and pubs and the traditional *værtshuser* are much frequented by the locals. Beers, shots and snacks are roughly a third of regular café prices, and many places sell a small selection of *smørrebrød* (the Danish open sandwich) and maybe some *frikadella med kartoffelsalat* (Danish meatballs with potato salad). Among the most convivial are:

The Cockney Pub @ Maren Smeds Gyde 8 ☎ 86 19 45 77
ⓦ www.cockneypub.dk
Hunters Pub @ Frederiks Allé 97 ☎ 86 13 63 50
Kurts Mor @ Fredens Torv 7 ☎ 86 18 18 48 ⓦ www.kurtsmor.dk
Peter Gift @ M P Bruuns Gade 28 ☎ 86 12 01 63
ⓦ www.petergift.dk
Sherlock Holmes Pub @ Frederiksgade 76 ☎ 86 12 40 50
ⓦ www.sherlock-holmes.dk
Strandborg @ Strandvejen 2 ☎ 86 12 05 08
Værtshuset @ Nørre Allé 61 ☎ 86 18 04 05

ⓦ www.turbinehallen.dk), **Entré Scenen** (@ Grønnegade 93D
ⓦ www.entrescenen.dk), **Ridehuset** (@ Vester Allé 3
ⓦ www.kulturhusaarhus.dk) and NRGi Arena (see page 92).

Putative 007s should know that the city's only casino, **Royal Casino** (@ Store Torv 4 ⓦ www.royalcasino.dk), is located in the five-star Hotel Royal (see page 37).

There are some excellent cinemas here. All films are shown in their original language and have Danish subtitles. Cartoons and animations often run in both English and Danish. The best are:

BioCity (Off Strøget) ⓐ Skt Knuds Torv 15 ⓣ 70 13 12 11 ⓝ All routes to Banegårdspladsen

Cinemaxx ⓐ Bruuns Galleri, M P Bruuns Gade 25 ⓣ 70 12 01 01 ⓦ www.cinemaxx.dk ⓝ All routes to Banegårdspladsen

Metropol (In Trøjborg) ⓐ Tordenskjoldsgade 21 ⓣ 70 13 12 11 ⓝ Bus: 1 to Niels Juels Gade

Øst for Paradis (Art-house cinema in the Latin Quarter) ⓐ Paradisgade 7–9 ⓣ 86 19 31 22 ⓦ www.paradisbio.dk ⓝ Bus: 1, 6, 9, 11, 16 to Nørregade

🔺 *Stop for a refreshing beer at the popular Peter Gift bar*

Sport & relaxation

The sports culture in Aarhus is flourishing. The locals actively participate in a variety of activities, from tango dancing to handball and curling to bowling. There is no shortage of opportunities if you would like to get active while you're here.

SPECTATOR SPORTS

The NRGi Arena and NRGi Park are both found in Marselisborg Park in the south of the city (see page 92). The city's football team, AGF, and its successful handball team, Århus GF, have their home grounds here. Visit the website for a full listing of spectator events.

PARTICIPATION SPORTS

Dance is considered a participation sport here. The **Tango Akademiet** (**Tango Academy**) site lists the city's tango classes (ⓦ www.tangoakademiet.dk). **DGI Huset** motion centre offers all manner of tone- and muscle-building devices (ⓐ Værkmestergade 17 ⓣ 86 18 00 88 ⓦ www.dgi-huset.dk). For sculptors of the body beautiful, there are a couple of fitness centres: **Fitnessdk** (ⓐ Busgadehuset, Frederiksgade 25 ⓣ 86 20 89 00) and **Equinox Fitness** (ⓐ Nørrebrogade 22–30 ⓣ 86 12 79 77 ⓦ www.equinox.dk). If you prefer to swim, the best pool is **Århus Svømmestadion** in Frederiksbjerg (ⓐ F Vestergaards Gade 3 ⓣ 86 12 86 44 ⓦ www.svst.dk). In the north is the city's ice-skating rink **Århus Skøjtehal** (ⓐ Gøteborg Allé 9 ⓣ 86 10 42 19 ⓦ www.skojtehallen.dk). The only bowling alley is **Århus Bowlinghal** (ⓐ Eckersbergsgade 13–15 ⓣ 86 12 52 00 ⓦ www.aarhusbowlinghal.dk).

● *Ice-skating in front of the Rådhus*

RELAXATION

Walking is probably the most relaxing thing you can do in public in Aarhus, but if you prefer not to move at all, there are also a few places in the city where you can treat yourself to a facial or a foot massage. Try **Helle Thorup** (ⓐ Frederiksgade 35 ❶ 86 18 39 00 ⓦ www.hellethorup.dk) or **Xenobia** (ⓐ Park Allé 5 ❶ 86 12 03 10).

Accommodation

Most of the city's hotels are in the Inner City area, near all the major attractions. It's usually easy to find a room, and the tourist office, VisitAarhus Velkomstcenter, is most helpful (see page 135).

One interesting and unique alternative is the *kro*. These are usually found in villages outside town, so you'll need a car. Some are old, thatch-roofed farmhouses; others are country manor houses. Aarhus is surrounded by them – try ⓦ www.krohotel.dk or ⓦ www.weekendopholdet.dk

Camping is a good option if you're not perturbed by occasional changeability of the weather.

HOTELS

Havnehotellet £ At the entrance to Marselisborg Pleasure Harbour, this hotel has great views, huge rooms and pleasant service. ⓐ Marselisborg Havnevej 20 ⓣ 70 22 55 30 ⓦ www.havnehotellet.dk ⓝ Bus: 6 to Chr Flintenborgs Plads

Cab Inn ££ Located centrally and right on the river, Cab Inn offers affordable, clean accommodation. All rooms have a

---

PRICE CATEGORIES
Based on the average cost of a double room in the high season.
£ under 600kr   ££ 600–900kr   £££ 900–1,200kr
££££ over 1,200kr

shower, toilet, TV and telephone. ⓐ Kannikegade 14
ⓣ 86 75 71 00 ⓦ www.cabinn.dk ⓝ Bus: 3 to Skolebakken; train
to Skolebakken

Hotel Atletion ££ Located just 2 km (1¹/₄ miles) outside the city
centre in Frederiksbjerg, this is an ideal place to stay if you prefer
to be surrounded by nature. Clean, functional rooms.
ⓐ Stadion Allé 70 ⓣ 89 38 60 38 ⓦ www.hotelatletion.dk
ⓝ Bus: 18, 19 to Århus Stadion

Hotel Guldsmeden ££–£££ A dinky, 100-per-cent-organic hotel
that captures the atmosphere of the city – warm, friendly,
familiar and homely. ⓐ Guldsmedgade 40 ⓣ 86 13 45 50
ⓦ www.hotelguldsmeden.dk ⓝ Bus: 6, 9, 11, 16 to Nørre Allé

City Hotel Oasia £££ Aarhus's latest designer accommodation
offering comes in the form of this fully renovated hotel,
featuring light and airy rooms packed with the sort of cutting-
edge design you would expect in Scandinavia. ⓐ Kriegersvej 27
ⓣ 87 32 37 15 ⓦ www.hoteloasia.dk

Hotel Ferdinand £££ Located on lively Åboulevarden, the hotel
is close to all the main attractions. ⓐ Åboulevarden 28 ⓣ 87 32
14 44 ⓦ www.hotelferdinand.dk ⓝ Bus: all routes to
Banegårdspladsen

Hotel Royal ££££ Hotel Royal is the place to stay in the heart of
the city if you want to splash out. ⓐ Store Torv 4 ⓣ 86 12 00 11
ⓦ www.hotelroyal.dk

● *Villa Provence provides a romantic setting at night*

Villa Provence ££££ A super-slinky design hotel, with a warm, inviting atmosphere. Rooms are spacious, and you'll find it difficult to tear yourself away. Perfect for romance. ⓐ Fredens Torv 12 ❶ 86 18 24 00 Ⓦ www.villaprovence.dk Ⓝ Bus: 3, 7 to Havnegade

APARTMENTS

Aarhus City Apartments £££ A good way of keeping your costs down in pricey Aarhus is to stay at this apartment hotel. Sleeping up to six people, each of the suites and studios has its own fully equipped kitchen, Wi-Fi and cable TV. ⓐ Fredensgade 18 ❶ 86 27 51 30 Ⓦ www.hotelaca.dk

HOSTELS & SLEEP-INS

City Sleep-In £ Here you can choose between a hammock in a dormitory or a private double room. There is a TV room, an info café with a wireless Internet area, a basement café with a pool, a small yard with a barbecue and a communal kitchen and dining area. ⓐ Havnegade 20 ⓣ 86 19 20 55 ⓦ www.citysleep-in.dk ⓝ Bus: 3, 7 to Havnegade

DANHOSTEL Århus Vandrehjem £–££ The reputable, well-run Danhostel is outside the city centre but has good transport connections. Choose from a dorm, a shared room or a private room. ⓐ Marienlundsvej 10 ⓣ 86 21 21 20 ⓦ www.aarhus-danhostel.dk ⓝ Bus: 1, 6, 9, 16, 56, 58 to Marienlund

KRO
Aarslev Kro £££ Good facilities, warm friendly service and a great kitchen serving rustic Danish cuisine. ⓐ Silkeborgvej 900, Brabrand ⓣ 86 26 05 77 ⓝ Local bus: 52, regional bus: 113 to Aarslev Kro

CAMPSITES
Århus Camping In the northern part of Greater Aarhus, this has two-, four- or six-person cabins, an area for tents, and a separate space for caravans. ⓐ Randersvej 400 ⓣ 86 23 11 33 ⓦ www.aarhuscamping.dk ⓛ All year round ⓝ Bus: 3, 117, 118

Blommehaven Camping Located just south of the city centre in Højbjerg, this wonderful campsite neighbours Marselisborg Forest and has its own beach. ⓐ Ørneredevej 35, Højbjerg ⓣ 86 27 45 22 ⓦ www.camping-blommehaven.dk

For further hotel and accommodation listings, try ⓦ www.visitaarhus.com and www.hotel.dk

THE BEST OF AARHUS

Whether you are on a weekend break or a more extended stay in Aarhus, the city offers a variety of sights and experiences that should not be missed.

TOP 10 ATTRACTIONS

- **Den Gamle By (The Old Town)** Step back in time and visit reconstructions of some of Denmark's oldest buildings in the historic Old Town (see page 62).

- **ARoS Århus Kunstmuseum (Aarhus Art Museum)** An architectural wonder that's one of the biggest art galleries in northern Europe (see page 66).

- **Latin Kvarteret** Stroll around the funky Latin Quarter, making sure you pause for coffee at **Altura Kaffe** (ⓐ Graven 22 ⓣ 86 20 28 55) or a beer at Ris Ras (see page 75).

- **Riis Skov (Riis Forest)** Take the bus, walk or bike along the waterside up to Riis Forest. A great place for a beach hike or a frolic in the sea (see page 81).

- **Tivoli Friheden (Tivoli Amusement Park)** Enjoy a fun day out with the kids at this small amusement park just south of Frederiksbjerg (see page 95).

- **Marselisborg Slot (Marselisborg Palace)** Visit Queen Margrethe's beautiful summer residence and gardens (see page 92).

- **Nordre Kirkegård (Northern Cemetery)** Who said cemeteries weren't groovy? This one offers stunning gardens and fantastic views over the harbour (see page 81).

- **Århus Festuge** Aarhus's annual cultural orgy (see page 14).

- *Smørrebrød* Savour the traditional Danish open sandwich (see page 27).

- **Fresh fish, organic veg** Be sure to have a mouthwatering meal at one of the many cafés or restaurants serving the most scrumptious local produce, such as Raadhuus Kaféen (see page 72).

○ *A row of brightly coloured Aarhus houses*

Suggested itineraries

HALF-DAY: AARHUS IN A HURRY

Stick to Århus Midtby – this is where most of the major attractions
are. The buildings in front of the Musikhuset (see page 71) are
architecturally impressive. Pop into the ARoS Århus Kunstmuseum
(see page 66), and pick up some gifts. The main shopping street,
Strøget, leads you into the Latin Quarter, where you can find
several spots to have lunch or dinner and soak up the atmosphere.

1 DAY: TIME TO SEE A LITTLE MORE

Spend the morning in one of the museums found in Århus
Midtby. After lunching in the Latin Quarter, walk either along
the harbour or through Nordre Kirkegård (see page 81) up to Riis
Skov. Alternatively, head west out to Den Gamle By. In the

● *The tranquil setting of the old watermill at Den Gamle By*

evening take a walk to lively Frederiksbjerg and treat yourself
to a gourmet meal at Malling & Schmidt (see page 98) or eat at
any one of the cafés or restaurants found on Jægergårdsgade.

2–3 DAYS: TIME TO SEE MUCH MORE

The best plan is to purchase a two-day ÅrhusCard (see feature
box below). Some of the museums, such as Kvindemuseet
(Women's Museum, see page 69) and Vikingemuseet (Viking
Museum, see page 68), are small, so it's not unrealistic to
consider visiting three in one day. Others, such as ARoS and
Steno Museet (ⓐ C F Møllers Allé 2 ⓣ 89 42 39 75
ⓦ www.stenomuseet.dk), can easily take up half a day each.
Visit the beautiful grounds of Marselisborg Slot (Marselisborg
Palace, see page 92) and take a walk around the surrounding
parks and gardens.

LONGER: ENJOYING AARHUS TO THE FULL

If you're not pressed for time, make sure you take a trip out
of town to Ebeltoft or even spend a couple of days on Samsø.
Why not take a trip out to Bazar Vest (see page 46) and do
some high-octane shopping?

ÅRHUSCARD

This essential city pass gives free admission to some of the
city's key attractions, free transport on the yellow city
buses (see page 49) and free parking in the city centre.
See ⓦ www.visitaarhus.com for details.

Something for nothing

The Musikhuset is one of the best places to go to obtain an experience of great value for free (see page 71). This centre for performing arts is known for offering the greatest number of free events of all Aarhus's cultural institutions. There is no charge to wander around the building itself, which is a wonderfully bright space, perfect for freebie art exhibitions (which it frequently has, in the Balkon Galleri). The gratis performances usually take place at the weekend between 11.00 and 14.00. Århus Teater (see page 66) has also recently started to put on special free performances. Check websites or call for upcoming opportunities.

Aarhus believes that one way to ensure that art is accessible to all is to provide it for free, and many of its cultural projects benefit from state funding with just this purpose in mind. There are several galleries dotted around the city, particularly in the Latin Quarter, which do not charge entrance fees. This is a natural way to come into closer contact with the local creative minds. Many of the artists are themselves present and are happy to share their ideas with visitors and admirers of their work.

As you wander around the city, look out for the omnipresent street art. Particular favourites in Aarhus are paint balloons: artists fill balloons with paint and hurl them at walls – there are a number of splatterings around as well as a lot of authorised graffiti.

⬤ *An open-air concert near the Rådhus*

When it rains

Rain need not dampen your enthusiasm for Aarhus. If you don't have a car, the best option is to purchase a one- or two-day ÅrhusCard (see page 43). You can happily spend hours in ARoS art museum (see page 66), which is a stone's throw from the Musikhuset (see page 71) and Rådhus (Town Hall, see page 62). Both are well worth visiting if you are interested in architecture and design.

If you like to shop and fancy a trip out of town, jump on the bus to the suburb Braband and head to the huge **Bazar Vest** (ⓐ Edwin Rahrs Vej 32 ❶ 86 25 42 11 ⓦ www.bazarvest.dk ❶ 10.00–18.00 Tues–Sun, closed Mon ⓝ Bus: 5, 15, 18 to Bazar Vest). This fantastic covered market has over 70 different stalls selling all kinds of ethnic things: jewellery, food, clothes, soft furnishings, gift items and so on. There are also plenty of different types of restaurants and eateries; you will realise here how ethnically diverse Aarhus actually is.

If you prefer to stay in town, pop into either of the department stores Salling (see page 72) or **Magasin du Nord** (ⓐ Immervad 2–8 ❶ 86 12 33 00 ⓦ www.magasin.dk), which both have good cafés where you can enjoy lunch. Alternatively, head northwest, past the university, to **Storcenter Nord** (ⓐ Finlandsgade 17 ❶ 87 39 42 20 ⓦ www.storcenternord.dk ❶ 10.00–18.00 Mon–Thur, 10.00–19.00 Fri, 10.00–16.00 Sat, closed Sun ⓝ Bus: 7, 26 to Storcenter Nord), a large shopping centre just outside the city centre.

Aarhus is also the perfect city for café-hopping and people-watching. Start at Vadestedet, head up to Store Torv and Lille

Torv and round the day off in one of the many cafés in the Latin Quarter. Englen and Ris Ras are particularly fab.

If none of this takes your fancy, then maybe a rainy day is a good time to take part in one of the sporting or relaxation activities listed on page 34.

🔺 *Storcenter Nord is a good place to dodge any showers*

On arrival

TIME DIFFERENCE
Denmark follows Central European Time (CET). Daylight saving applies; the clocks go forward one hour on the last Sunday in March and back an hour on the last Sunday in October.

ARRIVING
By air
Århus Lufthavn (**Aarhus Airport** ⓐ Stabrandvej 24, Kolind ❶ 87 75 70 00 ⓦ www.aar.dk) is located approximately 40 km (25 miles) north of the city centre. A 'Flybus' (95kr each way, also payable in euros, dollars and pounds) runs according to scheduled flights,

---

IF YOU GET LOST, TRY ...

Excuse me, do you speak English?
Undskyld, taler du engelsk?
Ornskewl, tala do ehng-ehlsg?

How do I get to ...?
Hvordan kommer jeg til ...?
Vohdan komma yai ti ...?

Can you show me on my map?
Kunne de vise mig det på kortet?
Kooneh dee veeseh mai di por korrdeht?

---

making five stops (Skæring Havvej, Egå Havvej, Lystrupvej, Vejlby Centervej, Randersvej) outside the city centre and Universitetet (the university) in the city centre before reaching Århus Hovedbanegård (central station). The journey takes about 45 minutes, and tickets can be purchased on the bus.

By rail

Trains to Fredericia, Aalborg and Lindholm from Copenhagen central station (København H) all stop in Aarhus at the central station, **Århus H** (ⓐ Banegårdspladsen 1 ❶ 70 13 14 15). The central station is easily accessible for disabled passengers, with lifts to all platforms and good toilet facilities. If you have any special requirements, call the station in advance. ❶ For times see InterCity or InterCityLyn timetables at ⓦ www.dsb.dk

By road

The main bus station **Århus Rutebilstation** (**Århus rtb** ⓐ Fredensgade ❶ 86 12 86 22 ⓦ www.bus-info.dk ❸ Bus and tourist information 07.00–22.00 daily) is located next to the harbour. There are several operators that have routes to the Greater Aarhus area and further afield. These buses are all blue and are not particularly pram- or wheelchair-friendly. However, the local buses, which yellow in colour and run by Midttrafik, are. There are also several X-buses that run express routes to other parts of Jutland.

There are a few main roads that head straight into the city of Aarhus. Nearest the coast in the north is Granåvej, which will bring you into the city along the harbour. Anticlockwise, the next major road is Randersvej, which will take you to Nørrebrogade through

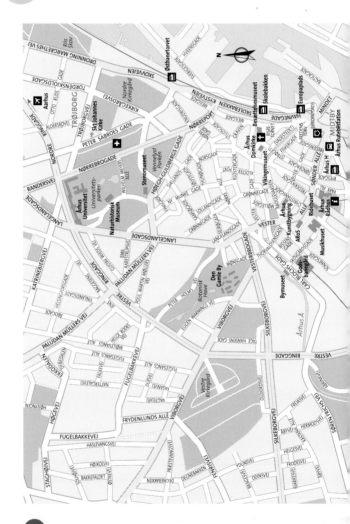

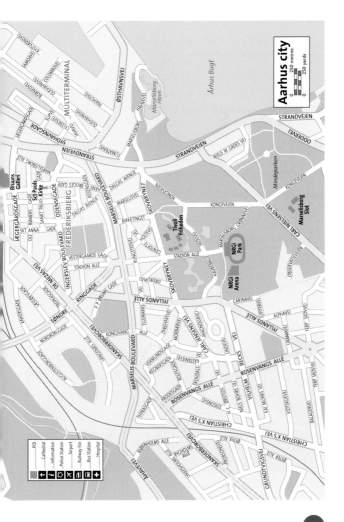

the university towards the harbour. Coming in from the northwest is Viborgvej, which takes you past Den Gamle By down to Vesterbrogade and Vester Allé. Coming in directly from the west is Silkeborgvej, which also takes you to Vesterbrogade. Finally, from the southwest is Skanderborgvej, which leads on to Frederiks Allé, taking you through the heart of the city.

By water
Århus Havn (Aarhus Harbour) is under development and may seem a touch basic. The Latin Quarter is located directly behind Skolebakken and Kystvejen, the main roads you are on when you leave the ferry.

FINDING YOUR FEET
As soon as you arrive in Aarhus you will feel a sense of familiarity. People are very friendly and used to foreigners; and you will struggle to find someone who doesn't speak English, so don't

⬥ *The roads curve around the harbour in Aarhus*

be afraid to ask questions. The Danes are still resisting the euro, but kroner are very easy to get used to. Traffic is on the right-hand side of the road and there is bicycle traffic, which has its own lights (like mini regular traffic lights). Pedestrian lights use the usual red and green men; if you cross on a red man, you risk being fined. Crime is rare in the city centre, but keep an eye on your belongings at all times and do not take unnecessary risks.

ORIENTATION

The heart of Aarhus centres around the harbour and is well organised, so streets are very easy to navigate. There are two crucial landmarks: the steeple of the Domkirke (cathedral, see page 58) can be seen from the harbour, the Latin Quarter and the main shopping street, Strøget; and the tower on the Rådhus (Town Hall, see page 62) is clearly visible from Frederiksbjerg, Århus H train station and the lower end of Strøget. The cathedral is located at the top of the main shopping street (with the main train station at the bottom), right next to the theatre and several of the smaller museums, and the Rådhus is located with the station to one side and a large green area on the other, which has the Musikhuset (see page 71), ARoS art museum (see page 66) and other cultural institutes forming its boundaries. The district of Frederiksbjerg starts directly south of the main train station. To the north of the city centre, past the Latin Quarter (which begins after you pass the cathedral heading north) you will find the University of Aarhus and Nordre Kirkegård (Northern Cemetery, see page 81). On its northern side are the Trøjborg district and its main street, Tordenskjoldsgade. Running parallel to this street, just one block away on the eastern side, you find the lower end

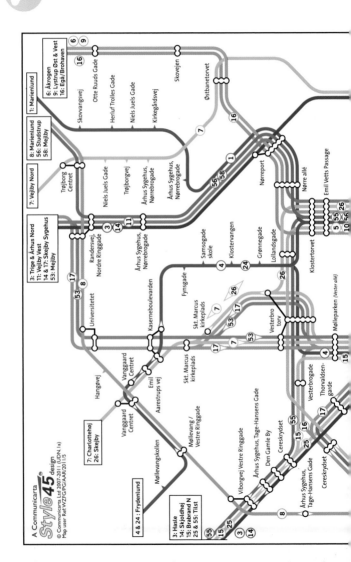

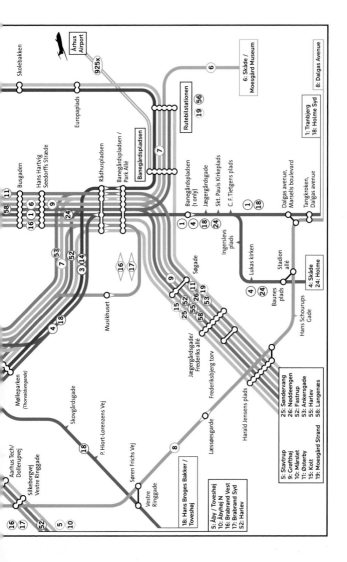

of Riis Skov, which overlooks the bay and has Aarhus's closest beach to its right.

The Århus Å (Aarhus River) flows from the west directly through the centre of the city to the harbour. The top end of Strøget (the part called Clemens Torv) actually forms a bridge over the newly opened riverside cafés on Åboulevarden (River Boulevard), known as Vadestedet. You can get down to the cafés via stairs, or turn left and left again at the cathedral, taking you along a street named Immervad.

GETTING AROUND

The easiest way to get around the centre of Aarhus is on foot, which is why we have listed some central locations without including public transport. However, for sights such as Marselisborg (see page 88), NRGi Park and Arena (see page 92) and Den Gamle By (see page 62), it is worth jumping on a bus. A detailed city map is available free from the tourist office (see page 135), the main bus station and the main train station.

All of the yellow city buses stop at the main train station, Århus H. Should you need a taxi, the best place to find one is the main train station at the bottom of Strøget: there are always plenty there.

Car hire

There are a couple of car-rental companies with offices in the city. Try **Europcar** (ⓐ Sønder Allé 35 ① 89 33 11 11) or **Avis** (ⓐ Jens Baggesens Vej 27 ① 86 16 10 99).

◗ *Half-timbered houses in Den Gamle By*

 THE CITY OF
Aarhus

Århus Midtby & the west

Neatly enclosed between the harbour and the ring road, Århus Midtby (the Inner City) is, like many areas of the city, easily tackled on foot (for locations where this is the case, this guide does not state public transport details). Art galleries, several museums, the theatre, the Musikhuset (Concert Hall), Rådhus, cathedral, the library, post office, bus station and main train station are all located in this pocket of town, as is the very cool Latin Quarter. If you're happy to brave a longer walk westwards, this will take you to the Botanic Gardens and one of Denmark's unique tourist attractions, Den Gamle By (see page 62). Or else, simply take the bus.

SIGHTS & ATTRACTIONS

Århus Domkirke (Aarhus Cathedral)

Construction started on this Gothic cathedral at the beginning of the 12th century. The building you see today was not completed until the beginning of the 16th century, and, at 93 m (305 ft) in length, it is the longest church in Denmark. It is also the church with the largest surface area of murals, many of which date back to the late 15th century (though one, painted around the so-called *spedalskhedsvindue* – leprosy window – in the northwest corner, dates from 1300). The interior is really quite stunning, and, if that were not enough, it has three organs. ⓐ Store Torv ① 86 20 54 00 ⓦ www.aarhus-domkirke.dk ① 09.30–16.00 Mon–Sat, closed Sun (May–Sept); 10.00–15.00 Mon–Sat, closed Sun (Oct–Apr) Ⓝ Bus: 3, 7, 14 to Skolebakken; train to Skolebakken

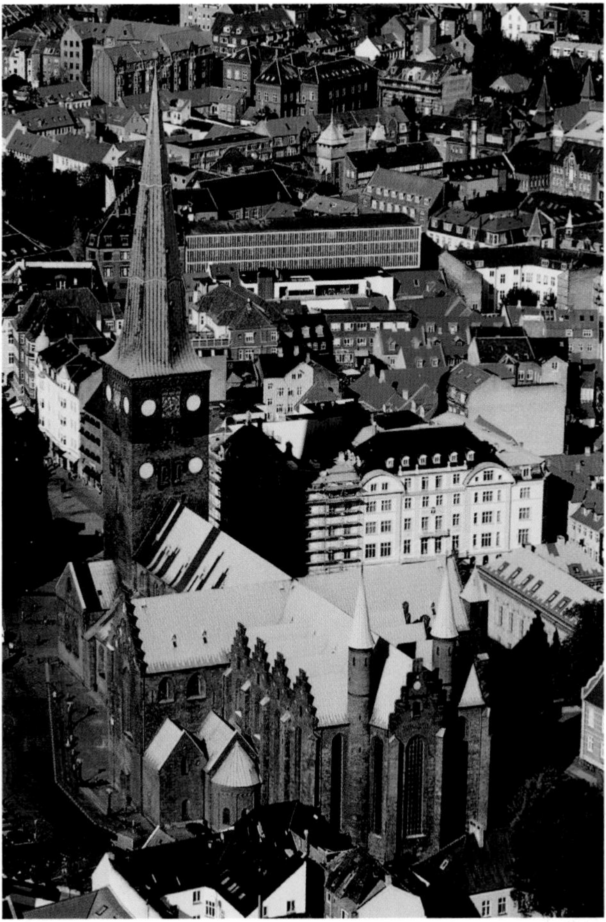

Aarhus's cathedral and view of the Latin Quarter

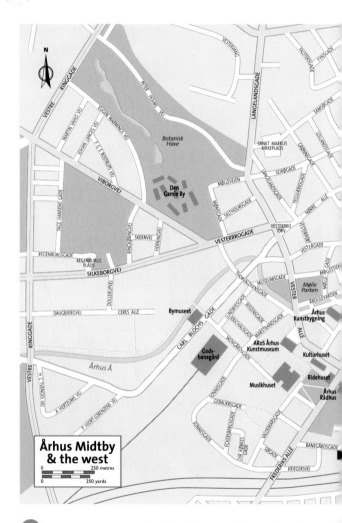

Århus Midtby
& the west

0 _____ 250 metres
0 _____ 250 yards

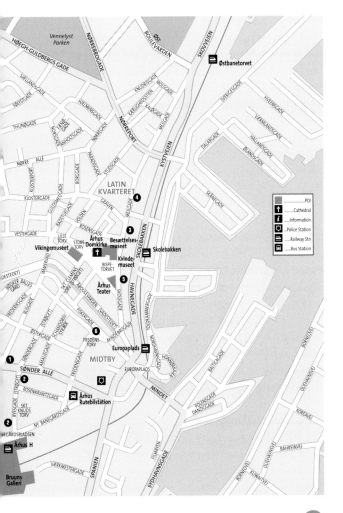

Vennelyst Parken

HØEGH-GULDBERGS GADE

NØRREBROGADE

ØST BOULEVARDEN

SKOVVEJEN

Østbanetorvet

SJÆLLANDSGADE

SØLVSTGADE

THUNØGADE

LANDS GADE

HJELMENSGADE

NØRREPORT

KNUDRISGADE

MOLSGADE

KARLBYGRESSTIEN

KALØGADE

MEJLGADE

SVERIGESGADE

HVEENSGADE

VÆRMLANDSGADE

HALLANDSGADE

ØLANDSGADE

KYSTVEJEN

DALARGADE

NØRRE ALLE

KLOSTERPORT

KLOSTERGADE

GULDSMEDGADE

BORGGADE

STUDSGADE

PALUDAN

GRAVEN

LATIN
KVARTERET ❹

SKANEGADE

VESTERGADE

BADSTUEGADE

VODEN

ROSENGADE

LILLE
TORV

STORE
TORV

Vikingemuseet

Århus
Domkirke ❸

Besættelses-
museet

Skolebakken

SKOLEBAKKEN

Kvinde-
museet ❺

HAVNEGADE

BISPE-
TORVET

SKT CLEMENS
TORV

Århus
Teater

BØRNER BALLES
GÅRD

FREDERIKSGADE

BISPEGADE

BUSGADE

ØSTERGADE

SCANDORFT-
STRÆDE

FISKERGADE

SCNDERGADE

MINDEGADE

TOLDKAMMERGADE

Europaplads

NØRRE HANEGADE

HONNØRQAJ

FREDENS
TORV ❻

MIDTBY

AMALIEGADE

FREDENSGADE

SØNDER ALLE

ROSENKRANTZGADE

EUROPAPLADS

MINDET

BALTICAGADE

SKT
KNUDS
TORV

Århus
Rutebilstation

NY BANEGÅRDSGADE

POLENSGADE

DANZIGGADE

HEGÅRDSPLADSEN

Århus H

VÆRKMESTERGADE

SPANIEN

SYDHAVNSGADE

FILMBYEN

Bruuns
Galleri

BONNEVEJ

OLIEHAVNSVEJ

KOREAVEJ

BAHREINVEJ

BONNEVEJ

OLIEHAVNSVEJ

KUWAITVEJ

	POI
✝	Cathedral
i	Information
🛡	Police Station
🚉	Railway Stn
🚌	Bus Station

Århus Rådhus (Town Hall)

This protected building, opened in 1941, was designed by the renowned Danish architects Arne Jacobsen and Erik Møller. The famous furniture designer, Hans J Wegner, joined the duo in designing the interior, furniture and other small details around the building. What is most visibly impressive is its symmetry – take a walk up the stairs to the fourth floor and look down. The 60-m (197-ft)-tall tower, which was not part of the original plan, was added at the request of the locals and has now become a landmark. Rådhuspladsen 2 89 40 20 00 www.aarhus.dk 09.30–15.00 Mon–Fri, closed Sat & Sun Bus: all routes to Banegårdspladsen

Botanisk Have (Botanic Gardens)

Locals enjoy the charming Botanisk Have in Aarhus as a regular park in which to sunbathe, read, walk, run and even sledge when the snow comes. A stream runs through the park from the northwest under the Chinese bridge and on to the dam at Den Gamle By, where it goes underground and surfaces again as the river, Århus Å. The tropical greenhouse, under renovation until 2012, is well worth a visit. Eugen Warmings Vej 89 40 26 87 www.aarhus.dk Park always open Bus: 3 towards Hasle, 14 towards Skjøldhøj, 25 towards Tilst

Den Gamle By (The Old Town)

Aarhus's number-one tourist attraction. This wonderful, reconstructed Old Town breathes the history of Aarhus over the past 400 years, with everyone in traditional dress pretending to carry out the daily tasks that would have been typical of

⬥ *Detail of traditional houses in the open-air museum of Den Gamle By*

residents of an old Danish town from the late 1500s to the 1920s. The town hosts the **Dansk Plakat Museum (Danish Poster Museum** ❷ Ludvig Feilbergsveg 7 ❶ 86 15 33 45 ⓦ www.plakatmuseum.dk), **Det Danske Urmuseum (The Danish Clock Museum)** and has a big **Lejetøjsmuseum (Toy Museum)**. Visit the tractor sheds, the local grocery store, the baker, the bookshop, the ironmonger and many other shops and places of work. There is an abundance of activities for children to take part in and a rather tempting sweet shop where they can help make the confectionery. This is a great place to visit at Christmas.

◗ *Quaint Møllestien is a peaceful haven in the city*

Between Easter and Christmas it is high season and there are always special events and exhibitions, particularly during Århus Festuge. ⓐ Viborgvej 2 ⓣ 86 12 31 88 ⓦ www.dengamleby.dk
ⓝ Bus: 3, 14, 25 to Den Gamle By ⓘ Admission charge

Møllestien (Mill Lane)

Møllestien is known as the most beautiful street in Aarhus. Most of its houses date back to the 18th century; the colourful façades, cobbled road and pretty flowers in hanging baskets give you the feeling of being in a small Danish village. Archaeological excavations revealed pottery dating back as far as the Middle Ages outside No 53, where – surprise, surprise – you can now buy classical Danish pottery items.

CULTURE

Århus Kunstbygning (Aarhus Centre for Contemporary Art)

This original, wonderful exhibition space was completed at the beginning of the 20th century. The aim of the Kunstbygning (which translates as 'Art Building') is to house a whole range of artistic expression from painting, sculpture and photography to performance, film and video. There are different exhibitions more or less every two months, and the venue is popular among up-and-coming Århusian creative talents. There are also often classical, jazz, rhythmic and electronic music concerts held here.
ⓐ J M Mørks Gade 13 ⓣ 86 20 60 50 ⓦ www.aarhuskunstbygning.dk
ⓛ 10.00–17.00 Tues & Thur–Sun, 10.00–21.00 Wed, closed Mon
ⓝ Bus: 5, 6, 7, 9, 10, 11 to Østergade ⓘ Guided tours in English upon request

Århus Teater (Aarhus Theatre)

Even if you don't see a performance, you shouldn't miss this beautiful protected building from 1900. With pretty, flowered, stained-glass windows and flora and fauna designs on the arched ceilings, it was designed by Hack Kampmann, the brains behind several prominent buildings in Aarhus, including Queen Margrethe's summer residence, Marselisborg Slot (see page 92). The swan ceiling in the main auditorium is a sight to behold. Tours of the theatre are held for the public on the first Saturday of the month during the theatre season (🕒 Sept–Dec). 🄰 Teatergaden ☎ 89 33 23 00 🆆 www.aarhusteater.dk 🕒 Doors open half an hour before the start of the performance Ⓝ Bus: 3, 7, 14 to Skolebakken; train to Skolebakken ❶ Admission charge

ARoS Århus Kunstmuseum (Aarhus Art Museum)

Big is meaningful at this international art museum, which opened in 2004. Its 17,700 sq m (190,550 sq ft) are divided up over nine floors, making one of northern Europe's largest museums. There are three galleries with permanent exhibitions displaying art from 1770 up to the present day, and a gallery on the ground floor specially designed for light and video installations. As well as housing the world's largest Per Kirkeby collection, ARoS features international artists such as James Turrell, Miwa Yanagi and Gilbert & George. There is also a fantastic junior museum with a workshop for the kids, a novel gift shop right at the entrance, **ART Restaurant** on the eighth floor (🕒 10.30–15.00 Tues & Thur–Sun, 10.30–21.00 Wed), and **ART Café** on the ground floor (🕒 10.00–16.45 Tues & Thur–Sun, 10.00–21.45 Wed). 🄰 Aros Allé 2 ☎ 87 30 66 00 🆆 www.aros.dk

◔ *The wonderful winding staircase at ARoS*

🕐 10.00–17.00 Tues & Thur–Sun, 10.00–22.00 Wed, closed Mon
🚍 Bus: 3, 4, 14, 16, 17, 18, 25 to Ridehuset ℹ Admission charge,
under 18s free

Besættelsesmuseet (Occupation Museum)

A suitably dignified museum that tells the history of Aarhus during
the German occupation between 1940 and 1945. Artefacts from the
Nazi and Danish military, propaganda, documents, posters and
other memorabilia from that time are displayed in the former Town
Hall and police station. 🔂 Mathilde Fibigers Have 2 📞 86 18 42 77
🌐 www.besaettelsesmuseet.dk 🕐 11.00–16.00 Sat & Sun (Jan & Dec);
11.00–16.00 Tues–Sun (June–Aug) 🚍 Bus: 3, 7, 14 to Skolebakken; train
to Skolebakken ℹ Admission charge, under 18s free

VIKINGEMUSEET (VIKING MUSEUM)

It's good to be reminded that, despite what it says in the
films, Vikings weren't just a bunch of pillagers, plunderers
and practitioners of non-consensual sex. This tiny, unique
museum, located in the basement under Nordea Bank,
gives a comprehensive history of the city when it was still
called 'Árós' and, in doing so, reveals that the Vikings were
organised administrators, skilled craftspeople and expert
navigators. Several of the pieces displayed here were
excavated at this precise location. 🔂 Skt Clemens Torv 6
📞 Moesgård Museum 89 42 11 00 🌐 www.vikingemuseet.dk
🕐 10.00–16.00 Mon–Wed & Fri, 10.00–17.30 Thur, closed Sat
& Sun 🚍 Bus: 3, 7, 14 to Skolebakken; train to Skolebakken

Bymuseet (Town Museum)

The Bymuseet is the ideal place to get a comprehensive overview of the history of the Greater Aarhus region since post-Viking days. The building itself is of historic and architectural significance, with the original part being the old Hammel station house. A new part of the building was designed to maximise the green area situated at the rear. An interesting and striking combination of panes of glass and wood panelling create the other face of Bymuseet. ⓐ Carl Blochs Gade 28 ⓣ 86 13 28 62 ⓦ www.bymuseet.dk ⓛ 10.00–17.00 Thur–Tues, 10.00–20.00 Wed ⓝ Bus: 18 to Skovgårdsgade ⓘ Admission charge, under 18s free

Kulturhuset (Culture House)

The aim of Kulturhuset is to give local artists a professional environment in which to work. The building houses advisers, teachers, workshops and studios. **Ridehuset**, which is run by Kulturhuset, is currently used to house *loppemarkeder* (flea markets), concerts, theatre productions, trade fairs and so on, and is therefore considered an important venue in Aarhus's cultural life. It is the perfect location for some of Aarhus's major cultural events (see Annual events, page 8). Brobjergskolen (ⓐ Frederiks Allé 20) is also part of the Culture House and is home to one of the city's dance schools. ⓐ Vester Allé 3 ⓣ 89 40 99 35 ⓦ www.kulturhusaarhus.dk ⓝ Bus: 3, 4, 14, 16, 17, 18, 25 to Ridehuset

Kvindemuseet (Women's Museum)

It should come as no surprise that the country with a solid reputation for gender equality has its own Women's Museum. This wonderful, tiny institution pays homage to the female of the

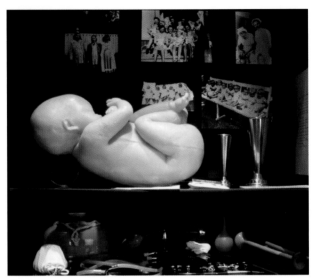

○ *Childbirth on display at the Kvindemuseet*

species by covering themes of childbirth, work, education and daily life. With small displays it presents a history of women from prehistoric times to the present day and features prominent Danish women who played a significant role in the feminist movement of the 1970s. There is also the very popular **Barndommens Museum (Childhood Museum)** here, and the cosy little café is well worth a visit. ⓐ Domkirkepladsen 5 ⓣ 86 18 64 70 ⓦ www.kvindemuseet.dk ⓛ 10.00–17.00 Thur–Tues, 10.00–20.00 Wed (June–Aug); 10.00–16.00 Tues & Thur–Sun, 10.00–20.00 Wed, closed Mon (Sept–May) ⓝ Bus: 3, 7, 14 to Skolebakken; train to Skolebakken ❶ Admission charge, under 18s free

Musikhuset (Concert Hall)

The stats say it all: this cultural institute attracts over half a million visitors every year. It brings together three of the city's major performing arts groups: the Aarhus Symphony Orchestra performs in the Symfonisk Sal; Filuren (the children's theatre group) runs a school for kids and puts on performances for adults and children; Det Jyske Musikkonservatorium's (Jutland's Music Academy, see page 20) 290 students and 70 staff are gathered in the Rytmisk Sal. Famous names such as Liza Minelli, Tina Turner and Sting have all performed here. Musikhuset is open to the public and often has free art exhibitions on the balcony. Just wander around and admire the wonderful bright spaces, comparing the old glass building from the 1980s with the modern extension behind the ticket office (notice the small room above the ticket office where Queen Margrethe sits during the intermission), or grab a bite to eat at one of the three restaurants. The gardens in front of the Concert Hall, known as Musikhusets Parken, are also quite special, having been designed to be enjoyed and navigated by all, particularly people with disabilities, and with visual and hearing difficulties. Different features such as paving stones, water features and aromatic flora and fauna are dotted around. ⓐ Thomas Jensens Allé ⓣ 89 40 40 40 ⓦ www.musikhusetaarhus.dk ⓛ Foyer & tickets 11.00–18.00 daily (June–Aug); 10.00–21.00 daily (Sept–May) ⓝ Bus: 3, 4, 14, 16, 17, 18, 25 to Ridehuset

RETAIL THERAPY

Box de Lux Specialising in stylish storage, this delightful boutique sells boxes and knick-knacks for the home. A great place for

designer gifts. ⓐ Graven 24 ⓣ 86 12 60 04 ⓦ www.boxdelux.dk
ⓛ 10.00–17.30 Mon–Fri, 10.00–15.00 Sat, closed Sun

Junk de Luxe Great Århusian designer clothes shop, particularly for
men, with customised second-hand clothing. ⓐ Studsgade 2–4
ⓣ 86 12 90 00 ⓦ www.junkdeluxe.dk ⓛ 11.00–18.00 Mon–Thur,
11.00–19.00 Fri, 10.00–15.00 Sat, closed Sun

Salling A pleasant department store famed for its high-
quality standards and good atmosphere. As well as a great
supermarket, Salling Super, in the basement, the store
houses over 35 retailers selling clothing, shoes, perfume,
books, toys and household wares. ⓐ Søndergade 27
ⓣ 86 12 18 00 ⓦ www.salling.dk ⓛ 09.30–18.00 Mon–Wed,
09.30–20.00 Thur & Fri, 09.00–17.00 Sat, closed Sun

TAKING A BREAK

Raadhuus Kaféen £ ❶ Everything here is traditionally
Danish. Lots of meat and fish, but not much for vegetarians.
ⓐ Sønder Allé 3 ⓣ 86 12 37 74 ⓦ www.raadhuus-kafeen.dk
ⓛ 11.00–23.00 Mon–Sat, 12.00–22.00 Sun, kitchen closes
one hour earlier

Sigfreds Kaffebar £ ❷ Great little coffee bar and snackerie.
Drink in or take away at either of the two bars in Ryesgade.
At No 3 the coffee bar is located in the wonderful Vangsgaards
bookshop – very relaxing atmosphere. ⓐ Ryesgade 28 &
Ryesgade 3 ⓣ 86 18 08 19/86 18 08 16 ⓦ www.sigfreds-

kaffebar.dk 🕒 (No 28) 08.30–18.30 Mon–Thur, 08.30–20.00 Fri, 09.30–18.00 Sat, closed Sun; (No 3) 10.00–17.30 Mon–Thur, 10.00–19.00 Fri, 10.00–16.00 Sat, closed Sun

Il Mercatino ££ ❸ A delightful Italian restaurant and deli that sells fantastic sandwiches. ⓐ Mejlgade 18 ☎ 86 12 00 48 ⓦ www.ilmercatino.dk 🕒 10.00–17.30 Mon–Fri, 10.00–14.00 Sat, closed Sun

🔺 *Pasta galore at Il Mercatino*

AFTER DARK

RESTAURANTS

Pihlkjaer ££ ❹ This brand new gourmet restaurant, a short stroll from the cathedral, serves up finely crafted vegetarian fare, fresh fish and imaginative meat dishes in cosy surroundings. ⓐ Mejlgade 28 ❶ 86 18 23 30 ⓦ www.pihlkjaer-restaurant.dk ⓛ 17.30–22.30 Tues–Thur, 17.30–23.30 Fri & Sat, closed Sun & Mon

Teater Bodega ££ ❺ Lively restaurant and bar frequented by actors and artists. Photographs and posters line the walls, telling the history of Aarhus's theatre scene. ⓐ Skolegade 7 ❶ 86 12 19 17 ⓦ www.teaterbodega.dk ⓛ From 11.30 Mon–Sat, kitchen 11.30–22.30 Mon–Sat, closed Sun

Restaurant Mellemrum ££–£££ ❻ A lovely restaurant located away from the busier parts of the city centre that prides itself on simple, modern dishes from the French kitchen. Limited menu with only three starters, main courses and desserts, but service is excellent. ⓐ Fredens Torv 2 ❶ 86 17 18 38 ⓦ www.restaurantmellemrum.dk ⓛ From 17.00 Mon–Sat, closed Sun

BARS & CLUBS

Bryggeriet Sct Clemens This microbrewery near the cathedral serves at least three types of ale cooked up on the premises to wash down the meat-heavy menu. The beer of the month can be anything from a sweet cherry concoction to a cloudy

wheat beer. ⓐ Kannikegade 10–12 off Skolegade ⓣ 86 13 80 00
ⓦ www.bryggeriet.dk ⓛ 11.30–24.00 Mon–Wed, 11.30–02.00
Thur–Sat, closed Sun

Café Smagløs One of Aarhus's liveliest cafés and music
venues, with a uniquely relaxed atmosphere. ⓐ Klostertorvet 7,
off Guldsmedgade ⓣ 86 13 51 33 ⓦ www.smagloes.dk ⓛ 09.30–
24.00 Mon–Thur, 09.30–03.00 Fri & Sat, 09.30–23.00 Sun

Ris Ras Filliongongong Fantastic, relaxing local bar serving
over 100 different beers. It does not serve food, but you are
welcome to bring your own and eat it here, smoke a water
pipe or play a board game with friends. ⓐ Mejlgade 24
ⓣ 86 18 50 06 ⓦ www.risras.dk ⓛ 12.00–02.00 Mon–Sat, 16.00–
24.00 Sun

Studenterhus An important student institution that's
housed in Pakhuset by the harbour, and is open to the general
public. Live music three times a week, nightly DJ and bar.
ⓐ Nordhavnsgade 1 ⓣ 86 18 30 21 ⓦ www.studenterhusaarhus.dk
ⓛ Check website for details, reception 14.00–16.00 Mon–Thur,
10.00–14.00 Fri, closed Sat & Sun

Under Masken Another institute in Aarhus's pub/bar life popular
with artists and actors. Worth a visit just to see the freaky masks
and theatre memorabilia bringing the walls and ceilings alive.
ⓐ Bispegade 3, off Rosensgade ⓣ 86 18 22 66 ⓛ 12.00–02.00
Mon–Sat, 12.00–24.00 Sun

Trøjborg & the north

To the northern side of the city centre are many important cultural sights such as the Stenomuseet, the Naturhistorisk (Natural History) Museum, the University of Aarhus, several other academic institutes and the beautiful Vennelyst Parken (see page 83). To the north of these is the residential district of Trøjborg. Like Frederiksbjerg, Trøjborg has a life of its own that's quite separate from that of Aarhus. Being in such close vicinity to the higher education institutes makes this a popular district among the students who constitute two-thirds of all the inhabitants of Trøjborg. Not surprisingly, the atmosphere here is decidedly laid-back and relaxed. In 2000, Aarhus municipality, with support from the By- and Boligministeriet (Ministry for Towns and Housing), set aside an astounding 10 million kroner for the further development of housing and garden areas here and for making improvements to the infrastructure and cultural and community life of Trøjborg. Much of this is now in place.

SIGHTS & ATTRACTIONS

Danmarks Japanske Have (Denmark's Japanese Garden)

A 20-minute bus journey north of Aarhus takes you to one of Denmark's most distinctive and prestigious international attractions. This highly original concept brings together all of the attributes Japanese culture is most famed for (except for sushi). Once within the gates you can take a peaceful walk around the beautiful Zen Garden. With a multitude of different

⬥ *Denmark's Japanese Garden*

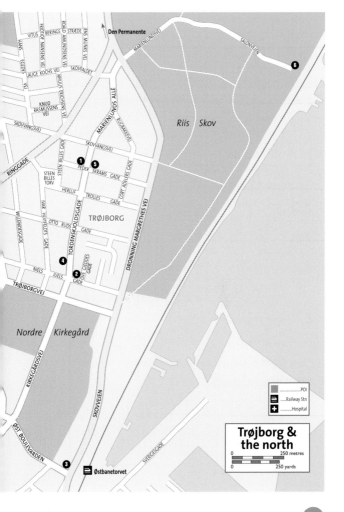

types of flowers and trees, including bamboo and bonsai, the scents and sights here can be savoured all year round. If you are partial to Japanese design, check out Zen Room. This design store is paradise for those looking for that unique something extra for the interior or exterior of the home. You'll find designer furnishings, garden furniture, pieces of art and various textiles, all produced with environmental awareness in mind and all free of artificial products. Zen Bath Wellness Centre is the place to go to find that sometimes elusive inner peace. Take an aromatherapy spa bath, have a full-body massage or, if you feel adventurous, try the hot-stone massage. There are plenty of different options and packages to choose from. Last, but far from least, you can give your taste buds a treat at Restaurant WH, named after one of Denmark's most celebrated chefs, Wassim Hallal. Strangely enough, this six-star restaurant does not serve Japanese food, but rather takes advantage of the high-quality Danish produce that can be found in this part of Jutland. ⓐ Randersvej 395, Trige ⓣ 72 20 08 89 ⓦ www.danmarksjapanskehave.dk ⓥ Regional bus: 117 from the central bus station to Trige, Randersvej/Østermøllevej

DEN PERMANENTE

On the beachside of Riis Skov you will find this old-fashioned public bathing area. There are shower facilities and, down at the beach, there are some separate bathing areas for men and women; this stretch is famous for its nature-loving nude bathers. ⓐ Strandvej 2, Riis Skov ⓥ Bus: 1, 6, 8, 16, 56, 58

Riis Skov (Riis Forest)

In the 1800s this forest became the private property of the monarchy. This meant that Århusianers could only use it for pleasure – they were forbidden to work on it. To this day the forest's main function is that of recreation, with two hiking routes mapped out, a wonderful youth hostel, a playground for the kids, and the bathing area down by the bay and the wonderful restaurant Sjette Frederiks Kro (see page 87). The forest has mainly birch and oak trees, many of which are over 150 years old. Ash and maple trees can also be found. There are four stones/rocks of great importance in the forest: one is from a meteorite that exploded over Denmark in 1951, and the other three are memorials to Queen Margrethe. ⓐ Dronning Magrethes Vej/Grenåvej ⓝ Bus: 6, 9, 16 to Riis Skov

Skt Johannes Kirke & Nordre Kirkegård
(St John's Church & Northern Cemetery)

The church in Aarhus is no different from any of the other institutes in the city: Skt Johannes Kirke actively joins in the city's cultural events such as Århus Festuge and the Jazz Festival, and encourages members of the parish to participate in events by giving them a little twist. It welcomes students to discuss films with religious and ethical content; it holds a 'Service and Spaghetti' evening (ⓛ First Tues of the month (May–Sept)) and an 'Open House' (ⓛ 14.00–16.30 Thur).

The nearby cemetery, Nordre Kirkegård (Northern Cemetery), is one of the most used green areas in the city of Aarhus. It dates back to 1876 and was originally opened due to lack of space in Søndre Kirkegård (Southern Cemetery) in the south of Aarhus.

◯ *Amphitheatre in the park at Århus Universitet*

This plot put the 'No Vacancies' sign up after just 42 years, and so came Vestre Kirkegård (Western Cemetery) to the west of the city. With numerous rare varieties of flora and fauna, the Nordre Kirkegård has a park-like feel and is often used as a place of rest for the living Århusianers. Look out for the exquisite statues and monuments dotted around the place. ⓐ Kirkegårdsvej 26 ⓘ 89 40 27 65 Ⓝ Bus: 1 to Kirkegårdsvej

Universitetsparken (University Park)

Just behind Vennelyst Parken and opposite Århus Sygehus (Aarhus Hospital) is University Park, home to **Århus Universitet** (**University of Aarhus** ⓐ Nordre Ringgade 1 ⓘ 89 42 11 11 Ⓦ www.au.dk), Stenomuseet (Steno Museum, see page 84), the Statsbibliotek (the State Library) and the Naturhistorisk Museum (Natural History Museum, see page 84). With its two lakes, this area is another fabulous place to stop for a break, though it's a little busier than some of the other chill-out zones since it is the heart of the university. ⓐ Nørrebrogade Ⓝ Bus: 3, 11, 56, 58, 90 to Nørrebrogade

Vennelyst Parken (Vennelyst Park)

A delightful park that used to be the grounds of the Århus Kunstmuseum. At present the Syplejehøjskole (Danish Nursing School) has its HQ here. The park itself is a great place to take your sandwich and relax during a busy sightseeing day, and is popular with birdwatchers and nature lovers. The park hosts the **Århus Middelaldermarked** (see page 11) at midsummer and other cultural events during the year. ⓐ Høegh-Guldbergs Gade Ⓝ Bus: 3, 11, 56, 58, 90 to Nørrebrogade

CULTURE

Naturhistorisk Museum (Natural History Museum)

The Natural History Museum's exhibits reflect the bent of its research department, and that is concentrated on entomology, freshwater ecology, the ecosystem, fauna and bioacoustics. It's a good idea to check the website to find out what the exhibition is at the time of your visit. ⓐ Wilhem Meyers Allé 210 ⓣ 86 12 97 77 ⓦ www.naturhistoriskmuseum.dk ⓒ 10.00–16.00 Sat–Thur, 10.00–14.00 Fri ⓝ Bus: 3, 11, 56, 58, 90 to Nørrebrogade ⓘ Admission charge, under 18s free

Stenomuseet (Steno Museum – History of Science & Medicine)

There are four sections to this undeniably fabulous museum. The History of Science is split into two sections, with a chronological exhibition stretching from the prehistoric times to the end of the 1600s and in which old telescopes, thermometers, barometers and other such apparatus make attractive exhibits. The other thematic exhibition covers astronomy and time, landscaping, optics, electromagnetism, nuclear physics, radio, arithmetic and chemistry. The History of Medicine's first floor has a chronological exhibition, which starts with an Egyptian mummy and an overview of Egyptian medical procedures from as far back as 1000 BC. On the ground floor there are a number of rooms reconstructed to depict an old dentist's surgery, a hospital laboratory and an operating room. There is also a small planetarium and a lovely *urtehaven* (herb garden), with over 400 different herb species, which is well worth a visit. ⓐ Bldg 100, C F Møllers Allé, Universitetsparken ⓣ 89 42 39 75

ⓦ www.stenomuseet.dk ⓛ 09.00–16.00 Tues–Fri, 11.00–16.00 Sat & Sun, closed Mon ⓝ Bus: 3, 11, 56, 58, 90 to Nørrebrogade ⓘ Admission charge, under 18s free

RETAIL THERAPY

Tordenskjoldsgade is the principal street in Trøjborg for shopping, though the main reason for being in this street is really the cafés. For gifts, souvenirs, clothes and bits and bobs for the home it is best to head back into town through the cemetery (delicately, there) along Mejlgade to the Latin Quarter and Strøget.

Paustian Located in the station house, Østbanegård, by the harbour (that's what you call a Paustian fact), this renowned designer furniture house is well worth a browse for inspiration, even if the pieces are beyond your budget. ⓐ Skovvejen 2 ⓘ 86 20 89 89 ⓦ www.paustian.dk ⓛ 10.00–18.00 Mon–Fri, 10.00–15.00 Sat & Sun ⓝ Bus: 6, 7, 9, 16 to Østbanetorvet; train to Østbanegård

TAKING A BREAK

There are numerous cafés along Tordenskjoldsgade (ⓝ Bus: 1 to Niels Juels Gade). If you fancy a picnic in one of the parks or even the forest, try the baker's, **Bavinchi** (ⓐ Tordenskjoldsgade 18 ⓘ 86 16 84 43), and for cold cuts or some *smørrebrød*, look no further than the butcher, **Kød Hjørnet** (ⓐ Tordenskjoldsgade 66 ⓘ 86 16 80 87).

Dolce Vita £ ❶ A fantastic ice-cream and coffee shop that serves some imaginative coffee/ice-cream combinations. ⓐ Tordenskjoldsgade 81 ❶ 86 10 38 30 ⓦ www.dolcevitais.dk/presse.asp ❻ 12.00–18.00 daily (Mar–Oct)

Rohdes £ ❷ Very popular snack bar serving sandwiches, bagels and crêpes: eat in or take away. ⓐ Tordenskjoldsgade 32 ❶ 86 16 93 95 ⓦ www.caferohdes.dk ❻ 10.00–21.00 daily

● *Join the locals for a drink in the cafés on Tordenskjoldsgade*

Fredes Flyvende Tallerken £–££ ❸ A nice, bright café,
sandwich bar and takeaway by the harbour that's justly famous
for its chunky chips. ⓐ Østbanetorvet 2 ❶ 86 16 92 57
🅦 www.fredesflyvendetallerken.dk 🕒 11.00–21.00 Mon–Sat,
12.00–21.00 Sun Ⓝ Bus: 6, 7, 9, 16 to Østbanetorvet; train to
Østbanegård

AFTER DARK

Chez Tony £ ❹ Fantastic little family-run restaurant offering
reasonably priced Greek home cooking. ⓐ Tordenskjoldsgade 25
❶ 86 16 88 30 🅦 www.cheztony.dk 🕒 15.00–23.00 Mon–Fri,
closed Sat & Sun

Café Ziggy ££ ❺ Small, cosy restaurant and café serving
delicious snacks and sandwiches. ⓐ Tordenskjoldsgade 96
❶ 86 10 43 22 🅦 www.cafeziggy.dk 🕒 09.00–23.00 Mon–Wed,
09.00–24.00 Thur & Fri, 10.00–24.00 Sat, 10.00–22.00 Sun

Sjette Frederiks Kro £££ ❻ It is well worth the trek to dine
in this great restaurant, serving wholesome French country
dishes. In wintertime it's a nice place to drink a cup of hot
chocolate after a long walk in the forest. ⓐ Salonvejen 1, Riis
Skov ❶ 86 16 14 00 🅦 www.sjettefrederikskro.dk 🕒 From 11.00
Tues & Wed according to reservations Ⓝ Bus: 6, 9, 16 to Riis Skov
❶ Reservation is a must

Frederiksbjerg & the south

The area directly south of the train station is known as Frederiksbjerg. Those who live in this district do not really need to go into Århus Midtby unless it is for a special occasion, but of course as a visitor, you'll want to zip about all over the place. M P Bruuns Gade and Frederiks Allé are the two main streets; the former is rather more chic and trendy, with lovely cafés, delis, a gourmet greengrocer's, Kong Gulerod (King Carrot!) and boutiques. Frederiks Allé is perhaps a touch more downmarket, with lots of *bodegas*, second-hand bookshops, supermarkets and fast-food places. Connecting these two streets is the popular Jægergårdsgade (Bus: 4, 18, 24 to Jægergårdsgade), which is a hangout for Aarhus's 25- to 30-somethings. On the stretch between M P Bruuns Gade and Frederiks Allé, you will find a couple of Aarhus's best restaurants, several interior design shops, a few *værtshuser*, a great pizza place and some handy supermarkets. There is even an environmentally friendly hairdresser, **Birthe Gleerup** (Jægergårdsgade 63 86 12 20 03 www.birthe-gleerup.dk). Don't miss the fruit and veg market on Ingerslev Boulevard on Wednesdays and Saturdays near St Paul's Church.

SIGHTS & ATTRACTIONS

Marselisborg Havn (Marselisborg Harbour)

Marselisborg Harbour, developed during the early 1980s, is the main harbour for pleasure boats. Located just south of the somewhat less than attractive Multiterminal, there is space for

⬤ *Roses in full bloom in front of the beautiful Marselisborg Slot*

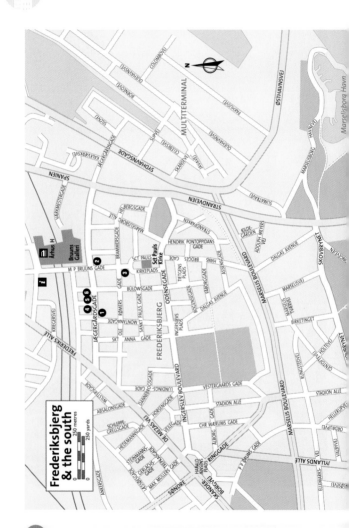

Frederiksbjerg
& the south

0 ____ 250 metres
0 ____ 250 yards

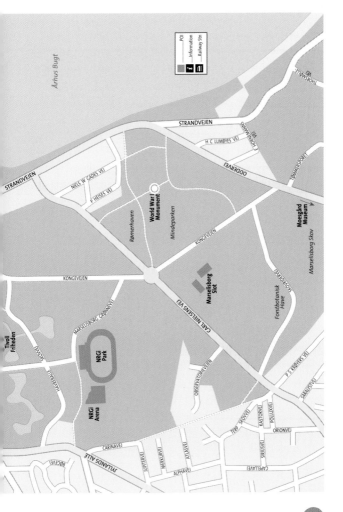

Arhus Bugt

POI
Information
Railway Stn

STRANDVEJEN

H C LUMBYES VEJ

E BØGH LAURSENS VEJ

ODDERVEJ

THORSMØLLE VEJ

STRANDVEJEN

NIELS W GADES VEJ

F HEGELS VEJ

Ramerhaven

World War I Monument

Mindeparken

KONGEVEJEN

EMMERSGÅRDSVEJ

Moesgård Museum

Marselisborg Skov

KONGEVEJEN

MARSELISBORG CARINAVEJ

Marselisborg Slot

Forstbotanisk Have

BARBOSOLVEJ

CARL NIELSENS VEJ

F S KRØYERS VEJ

Tivoli Friheden

PAXVEJ

HAVREVEJEN

NRGI Park

OBSERVATORIEVEJEN

SARDUSVEJ

NRGI Arena

TERP SKOVVEJ

KASTOVEJ

POLLUVEJ

ORIONVEJ

CARINAVEJ

CAPELLAVEJ

JYLLANDS ALLE

BÖGEVEJ

LUPINVEJ

MERKURVEJ

ATLASVEJ

ALPHAVEJ

up to 450 vessels here. This is the place to enjoy a beer or a tasty meal and soak up that special atmosphere found at sailing clubs the world over. As this is Aarhus, things are extremely informal, laid-back and relaxed. ➍ Marselisborg Havnevej 38 ➊ 86 19 86 44 ➍ www.marselisborghavn.dk ➍ Bus: 6 to Chr Flintenborgs Plads

Marselisborg Slot (Marselisborg Palace)

Unfortunately, this beautiful palace, currently used as the queen's summer residence, is not open to the public; but the grounds are. The building, constructed between 1899 and 1902 and designed by the Danish architect Hack Kampmann, was a gift to the Crown Prince Christian X and Princess Alexandrine, who at that time also used the palace as a

NRGI PARK

Take note, sports fans, for this is the sporting centre of Aarhus. With a capacity for 20,000 spectators, it is home to, among others, the city's scandalously underachieving football club, AGF (Århus Gymnastik Forening – try making a terrace chant out of that). NRGi Park and its arena are also popular venues for many different spectator sporting events, cultural events and big concerts (Cliff Richard, George Michael, Elton John and Depeche Mode have played here in recent years). ➌ Stadion Allé 70, Marselisborg Park ➊ 89 38 60 00 ➍ www.atletion.dk ➍ Bus: 18, 19 to Århus Stadion

summer residence. The park surrounding the palace was designed with an English garden in mind, hence the big lawns surrounded by trees. There are also a rose garden and herb garden, as well as some small statues and monuments. Marselisborg Skov, just south of the palace, is one of the older forests and it marks the beginning of a large forested area and deer park. The leafy forests in Aarhus are dominated by birch trees, almost a fifth of which are over 150 years old. The palace and surrounding gardens, parks and forest should not be missed if you are to fully appreciate the diversity of this wonderful city. ⓐ Kongevejen ⓦ www.kongehuset.dk ⓝ Bus: 1, 19 to Mindeparken

Mindeparken (Memorial Park)

A tranquil memorial park that commemorates the Danes who lost their lives in World War I, Mindeparken was inaugurated by King Christian X in 1925. Located to the south of Frederiksbjerg, next to Marselisborg Slot (see above), the park covers an area of 12 ha (30 acres). The monument, positioned right in the middle, consists of a circular limestone wall on which are carved war scenes alongside a list of the names of 4,140 deceased Danish soldiers. Also in the park is the Forstbotanisk Have, a large botanic garden housing over 900 different tree and bush types from all over the world. Look out for the two small buildings known as the Donbækhusene. These have seen a bit of life in their time, having been homes to the servants of Marselisborg, homes to the forest workers and a storage facility for gardening equipment. Be sure to visit the beautiful Rømerhaven (Roman gardens) as well. ⓝ Bus: 1, 19 to Mindeparken

Moesgård Museum

Just south of Marselisborg, along the coast, you will come to
Moesgård beach and the woods that envelop Moesgård Manor,
home to the archaeological and ethnographical Moesgård
Museum. This wonderful, family-friendly museum contains
ancient artefacts dating back to the Iron Age, many of which
were found in the nearby Illerup River valley. Its most famous
resident is the Grauballe man, the only completely preserved
bog-man in the world. The site also contains several reconstructed
Viking age houses, and there is a prehistoric pathway which takes
you through a reconstructed Iron Age house. There are also Stone
Age and Bronze Age graves and cult sites. ⓐ Moesgård Allé 20,
Højbjerg ❶ 89 42 11 00 ⓦ www.moesmus.dk ❹ 10.00–17.00 daily
(Apr–Sept); 10.00–16.00 Tues–Sun, closed Mon (Oct–Mar)
ⓝ Bus: 6 to Moesgård Museum ❶ Admission charge, under
18s free

● *Moesgård Manor, home to a fascinating museum*

Sct Pauls Kirke (St Paul's Church)

Built in 1880, the architecture of St Paul's Church, like the Domkirke, was inspired by Byzantine form. Heavy dark wood furnishing beautifully offsets the pretty, white interior and simple (yet decorative) ceilings. A wonderful peculiarity of this church is its altarpiece, the frame of which was made by a young woman who was still just an apprentice. The original crucifix, with a slender Christ sculpted from ivory, was stolen and then replaced in the 1960s. Every detail here tells a fascinating story, and the church combines 19th- and 20th-century architecture and design quite brilliantly. ⓐ Sct Pauls Kirkeplads ⓣ 86 12 21 54 ⓦ www.sctpauls.dk

Tivoli Friheden (Tivoli Amusement Park)

The city's only amusement park now has rides and attractions for adults, alongside treats for the whole family to enjoy together and plenty for the kids alone. It started its days in 1903 as a restaurant by the name of Friheden, and throughout the century developed gradually, being alternately used as a concert venue, a cultural meeting spot, a mini-golf course and, eventually, an amusement park. ⓐ Skovbrynet ⓣ 86 14 73 00 ⓦ www.friheden.dk ⓛ Hours vary greatly, check website for details ⓝ Bus: 4, 18, 24 to Friheden ⓘ Admission charge

RETAIL THERAPY

Frederiksbjerg has three main destinations that will attract shoppers: Jægergårdsgade is great for locally produced ceramics, interior design shops and music outlets; M P Bruuns Gade

(Bus: 4, 18, 24 to Jægergårdsgade) has some lovely food shops and kids' clothes shops; and Bruuns Galleri (shopping centre) has the usual high-street shops (clothes, sportswear, mainstream art, etc).

A Mano Known for its high-quality Moroccan leather cushions produced in Marrakesh, this warm, atmospheric shop is a pleasure to browse and get inspiration for your home. ⓐ Jægergårdsgade 53 ⓣ 86 12 31 50 ⓦ www.amano.dk ⓛ 10.00–18.00 Mon–Sat, closed Sun

Made in.... A wonderful children's clothing and toy store. Also stocks household items and decorative ornaments. ⓐ M P Bruuns

⬤ *Almost everything for the kids in Made in....*

Gade 35 ❶ 86 18 36 00 ⓦ www.madeinshop.dk ❶ 10.00–17.30
Mon–Thur, 10.00–18.00 Fri, 10.00–15.00 Sat, closed Sun

Marianne Røgild Quaint ceramics workshop and retail outlet,
selling sturdy, Danish-style earthenware. ⓐ Jægergårdsgade 55
❶ 86 76 15 76 ⓦ www.kunstruten.dk ❶ 12.00–17.30 Mon,
10.00–17.30 Tues–Fri, 10.00–13.00 Sat, closed Sun

TAKING A BREAK

There are numerous delightful cafés on Jægergårdsgade and
M P Bruuns Gade as well as a couple of eateries in Bruuns Galleri.

D's Sandwich & Pizza £ ❶ Delicious and extremely popular
pizzas and sandwiches with a Mediterranean twist. You can
eat in or take away, and things get very busy at lunchtime.
ⓐ Jægergårdsgade 54 ❶ 73 72 00 00 ⓦ www.dsandwich.dk
❶ 10.00–22.00 daily

Mademoiselle £ ❷ Toothsome sandwiches made with home-
made bread and fresh local ingredients. Organic smoothies and
juices. An extremely cosy little place. ⓐ M P Bruuns Gade 33
❶ 86 12 20 53 ⓦ www.mademoiselle.dk ❶ 11.00–19.00 Mon–Fri,
11.00–15.00 Sat, closed Sun

Schweizer Bageriet £ ❸ A delightful little bakery selling
delectable cakes, biscuits and beverages. ⓐ M P Bruuns Gade 56
❶ 86 12 34 47 ⓦ www.schweizerbageriet.dk ❶ 06.30–18.00
Mon–Thur, 06.30–19.00 Fri, 06.30–17.00 Sat & Sun

AFTER DARK

RESTAURANTS

Klassisk 65 ££ ❹ Small wine bar and bistro serving high-quality, uncomplicated, good food in a totally relaxed atmosphere with great, friendly service. Fantastic wine and cheese selection. ⓐ Jægergårdsgade 65 ❶ 86 13 12 21 ⓦ www.klassiskbistro.dk ⓛ 12.00–15.00, 17.30–late daily

Rarbar ££ ❺ A cosy café, restaurant and bar that serves great cocktails, good food and also has a DJ playing three nights a week. Check out the SupperClub on Saturday nights: a three-course meal, prepared by the city's trainee chefs, and a cocktail cost 150kr. ⓐ Jægergårdsgade 71 ❶ 86 19 60 80 ⓦ www.rarbar.dk ⓛ 11.00–01.00 Mon–Wed, 11.00–02.00 Thur–Sat, 11.00–18.00 Sun

Malling & Schmidt £££ ❻ One of Aarhus's best fine-dining restaurants, with award-winning chefs and the finest-quality raw ingredients. ⓐ Jægergårdsgade 81 ❶ 86 17 70 88 ⓦ www.mallingschmidt.dk ⓛ 18.00–24.00 Wed–Sat, closed Sun–Tues

VÆRTSHUSER (PUBS)

Some of Aarhus's oldest pubs are located in Frederiksbjerg. If you happen to be in Jægergårdsgade, pop into **Pub'en**, which has been there since 1972 (ⓐ Jægergårdsgade 62 ❶ 86 13 60 98) and the lively **Jægerhytten** (ⓐ Jægergårdsgade 61 ❶ 86 12 22 75).

◗ *The Sletterhage lighthouse has prime position at the seaside*

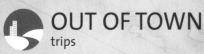

OUT OF TOWN
trips

The Djursland coastline: Aarhus to Ebeltoft

Aarhus lies on the southwestern border of the Djursland region, which is famous for its beaches and wonderful coastline, hilly countryside, forests and tourist attractions. The coastal route from Aarhus to Ebeltoft takes you through some lovely small towns and villages. Djursland is a popular destination for Danish tourists during the summer holiday and is covered with summer houses. At Rønde you can visit some of Denmark's most ancient ruins. Ebeltoft is probably the town which reflects the charm of the whole region most, with its cobbled streets and half-timbered houses and beaches.

GETTING THERE

The most enjoyable way to take this trip is by car. Just follow route 15 out of Aarhus (along Kystvejen and Skovvejen, past Riis Skov), and turn off at route 21 just after you pass Rønde. This road takes you to the heart of Ebeltoft on Strandvejen.

Alternatively, you can take the regional bus or train. Buses 120, 121, 122 and 123 from the **Rutebilstation** (@ Fredensgade ☎ 86 12 86 22 ⓦ www.midttrafik.dk) all stop in Følle and Rønde; there are frequent departures and the journey takes 45 minutes. From Aarhus to Ebeltoft take No 123; this departs daily every half-hour between 08.30 and 16.30, and once an hour until 21.30.

For detailed maps and further information on Djursland, contact the VisitAarhus Velkomstcenter located near the main

◤ *The town hall in Ebeltoft*

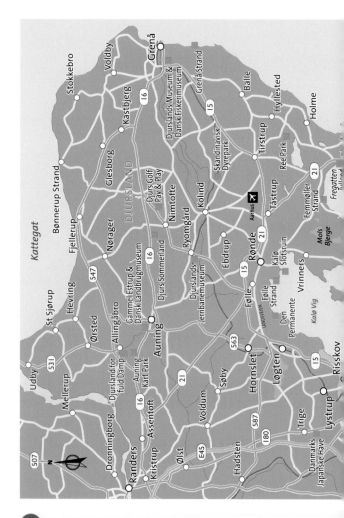

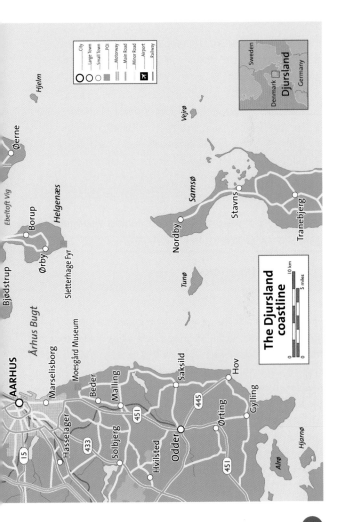

Hjelm

Øerne

Ebeltoft Vig

Borup

Helgenæs

Ørby

Sletterhage Fyr

Bjødstrup

Århus Bugt

Marselisborg

Moesgård Museum

Beder

Malling

AARHUS

Hasselager

Solbjerg

Hvilsted

Saksild

Hov

445

Ørting

Gylling

Odder

451

Alrø

Hjarnø

433

15

451

Vejrø

Samsø

Nordby

Stavns

Tranebjerg

Tunø

Sweden

Denmark

Djursland

Germany

City
Large Town
Small Town
POI
Motorway
Main Road
Minor Road
Airport
Railway

The Djursland coastline

0 ___ 10 km

0 ___ 5 miles

> **IF YOU DO LIKE TO BE BESIDE THE SEASIDE …**
>
> … Djursland is the place for you. With the sea on almost three-quarters of its borders, every beach here is a winner, especially Grenå Strand, Ebeltoft Strand, Følle Strand at Kalø and Femmøller Strand. And it's not just about setting up your deckchair and wearing your handkerchief as a hat – the coves at Ebeltoft and Kalø are particularly popular with surfers and divers and are surrounded by beautiful scenery.

train station (see page 135). Otherwise, contact **VisitDjursland** (☎ 87 52 18 00 ⓦ www.visitdjursland.com).

SIGHTS & ATTRACTIONS

Ebeltoft

Ebeltoft is officially the cleanest town in Denmark. In July and August you have the opportunity to join a free guided tour of this quaint little place, every Tuesday at 18.30 starting at Grisetorvet, or you could simply follow the nightwatchmen every evening as they take different routes keeping an eye on what's going on in the town. Adelgade is the main shopping street and is littered with 18th-century half-timbered buildings that uphold the spirit and simplicity of the Old Town.

The famous ***Fregatten Jylland*** (ⓐ Fregatøen ☎ 86 34 10 99 ⓦ www.fregatten-jylland.dk ⏰ 10.00–17.00 daily (Apr–June, Sept & Oct); 10.00–19.00 daily (July & Aug); 10.00–15.00 daily

🔺 *The wooden warship* Fregatten Jylland *is moored at Ebeltoft*

(Nov–Mar)), the so-called ship that would not die, is moored here. It is the longest wooden ship in the world, and after sailing as a war vessel, became the royal ship for several years. This is a fantastic place for children and there are special events throughout the year.

Ebeltoft Zoo and Safari Park, **Ree Park** (ⓐ Stubbe Søvej 15 ❶ 86 33 61 50 ⓦ www.reepark.dk ⓛ 10.00–17.00 daily (Apr–June & mid-Aug–Oct); 10.00–19.00 daily (July–mid-Aug)), is also a favourite with children. Another is **Jump'n'Fun** (ⓐ Erhvervsparken 2–4 ❶ 89 53 14 41), an indoor activity centre with climbing wall, table tennis, table football, board games, a pirate ship and loads more.

Ebeltoft has many fun cultural events throughout the year. In mid-October there is the **Ebelfestival** (❶ 86 34 38 55 ⓦ www.ebelfestival.dk), which allows visitors to taste, smell, look at and feel all sorts of different apples in many different forms.

When it comes to grapes, the people of Ebeltoft stick to the wine form and hold an annual wine festival, **Vinfestival** (ⓐ Ndr Strandvej 3 ❶ 86 34 33 00 ⓦ www.ebeltoftby.dk), on the first weekend in March. Wines from Europe, South America, Africa, the USA, Australia and New Zealand are on offer at Hotel Ebeltoft Strand, as well as in other restaurants and venues throughout the town.

The **Folkefestival** (ⓐ Fregatøen ❶ 86 34 00 33 ⓦ www.ebeltoft kulturhus.dk), held over three days on Ascension Day weekend in May, is one of Ebeltoft's annual music events. Popular Danish folk and jazz bands get together and perform live at the superb *Fregatten Jylland*. **Ebeltoft Open Air** is another, and this is held at the end of July on the beach.

There are two museums any visit to Ebeltoft should include. **Det Gamle Rådhus (The Old Town Hall** ⓐ Juulsbakke 1 ❶ 86 34 55 99 ⓦ www.ebeltoftmuseum.dk ❷ 11.00–15.00 daily (May, June & mid-Aug–Sept); 11.00–17.00 daily (July–mid-Aug); 11.00–15.00 Sat & Sun, closed Mon–Fri (Oct–Apr)), built in 1789 on the site of the original town hall, houses part of Ebeltoft Museum. The museum preserves the cultural artefacts that the town and neighbouring Rønde municipalities have inherited.

The stunning **Glasmuseet (Glass Museum** ⓐ Strandvejen 8 ❶ 86 34 17 99 ⓦ www.glasmuseet.dk ❷ 10.00–17.00 daily (Apr–June, Sept & Oct); 10.00–18.00 daily (July & Aug); 10.00–16.00 Tues–Sun, closed Mon (Nov–Mar)), in the old Customs and Excise building, opened an amazing new wing in 2006. This space has made room for a lovely café with views over the harbour, a bright exhibition space, a shop, reception and a glass-blowing studio where you can watch the artists at work.

▲ *The modern lines of the harbourside Glasmuseet*

The museum is home to a diverse collection of contemporary glass from all corners of the world; this is probably not a place to bring young children. In addition to the Glasmuseet, you will find several shops in town selling glassware, where the glass-blowers are more than happy to show off their skills.

To find out more about what's on in Ebeltoft contact tourist information **Ebeltoft Mols Turistinformation** located near *Fregatten Jylland* (see map on page 102) (ⓐ S A Jensens Vej ⓣ 86 34 14 00 ⓔ ebeltoft@destinationdjursland.dk).

Helgenæs

Nowadays, Djursland's southernmost point is largely uninhabited – the main reason for stopping here is to enjoy the views across the water to the neighbouring island of Samsø and to see Aarhus across the bay. There are two main lookout spots. The first, down

by the water, is the Sletterhage Fyr (Sletterhage Lighthouse), which dates back to 1872. The other lookout tower, at a higher elevation, is the Tyskertårn (German Tower), which was built by the Germans during World War II. ◎ Local bus: 361 from Rønde to Ørby

Mols Bjerge

The area of Mols is famous for the Mols Bjerge (Mols Mountains). These hills are as close as Denmark gets to mountains. The combination of absolute tranquillity and pretty scenery, with meadows and grazing cows on one side and the bay on the other, is something special. ⓦ www.skovognatur.dk ◎ Alight from the bus at Femmøller and take a local bus, or walk through Mols Bjerge

---

◐ *Rolling fields reach down to the sea in the region of Mols*

Rønde

If you want to visit one of Denmark's best-preserved medieval castle ruins, this old trading town located inland from the Kalø Vig inlet is the place to alight. **Kalø Slotsruin (Kalø Castle Ruins)** covers a large area with the main castle building on a piece of land jutting out into the sea. The land linking the island to the mainland is a medieval artificial construction, which is also amazingly well preserved. To get to Kalø Slotsruin turn down Kaløvej (towards Ebeltoft); stop at the big car park and

⬤ *Fishing boats moored at Kalø*

walk down to the ruins. Toilets, shop and information are all available here.

The woods in Kalø are of equally great historic importance. There are an astounding 100 or so ancient monuments dating from the Stone and Bronze Ages here.

Nowadays, the town of Rønde is dominated by more modern buildings, but still has a seaside village feel to it. If you don't have the energy to take a tour of the ruins and woods, then you can get a great view of it all from the recently renovated **Bregnet Kirke** (ⓐ Kirkebakken ❶ 86 37 27 09).

Rønde Turistbureau ⓐ Hovedgaden 10 ❶ 86 37 23 66
ⓦ www.visitdjursland.com

TAKING A BREAK

The best place to stop for a bite to eat in this area is Ebeltoft.

Café Bageriet £ Come here for a tasty, original light lunch.
ⓐ Adelgade 60 ❶ 86 34 10 71

Chokoladehuset £ If you fancy a sweet snack, make sure you pop into this bakery and *chocolaterie*. ⓐ Adelgade 19

Gryden £ Head to this cosy family-run restaurant for a traditional, inexpensive Danish lunch. ⓐ Adelgade 32 ❶ 86 34 13 00
ⓦ www.gryden.dk ❶ 10.00–21.00 Mon–Sat, 11.00–21.00 Sun

Mols og Fanø Bolsjer £ A quaint little confectioner. ⓐ Nedergade 11
❶ 86 34 66 55

AFTER DARK

Mellem Jyder ££ A delightful restaurant that maintains a historical ambience with its furnishings and produces high-standard traditional Danish meals using the best local ingredients. ⓐ Juulsbakke 3, Ebeltoft ⓣ 86 34 11 23 ⓦ www.mellemjyder.dk ⓛ 12.00–late daily

Restaurant Hyttefadet ££ A wonderful restaurant at Ebeltoft Harbour with an amazingly extensive fish and meat menu. ⓐ Havnevej 11A ⓣ 86 34 46 47 ⓦ www.restaurant-hyttefadet.dk ⓛ 12.00–late Wed–Sun, closed Mon & Tues

Restaurant Nils £££ Great for a gourmet dinner with good wines and excellent service. ⓐ Adelgade 62, Ebeltoft ⓣ 86 34 44 66 ⓛ 11.00–late Tues–Sat, closed Sun & Mon

ACCOMMODATION

Accommodation in this area is a little limited, so be sure to book in advance.

Danhostel Ebeltoft £ A cosy little youth hostel five minutes' walk from the centre of Ebeltoft and a short canter up from the beach. In the evenings you can snuggle up in front of the open fire or enjoy your meal in the pretty back yard. ⓐ Søndergade 43 ⓣ 86 34 20 53 ⓦ www.danhostel.dk

Danhostel Rønde £ A great youth hostel lurks within this lovely, half-timbered house; there are parking facilities,

⬤ *A solitary old farmhouse at Kalø*

and you can hire a bike here. ⓐ Grenåvej 10B ① 86 37 11 08
Ⓦ www.danhostel.dk

Ebeltoft Park Hotel £££ You could do a lot worse than choose
these very decent digs just back from the beach in Ebeltoft.
Rooms are well maintained, if a little unimaginative, and there's
a well-respected restaurant on the premises. ⓐ Vibæk Strandvej
4 ① 86 34 49 41 Ⓦ www.ebeltoftparkhotel.dk

Molskroen £££ Spoil yourself with beautiful views, tranquillity,
good food, wine and warm hospitality. The restaurant was voted
Denmark's 2006 Restaurant of the Year. Perfect for a romantic
weekend away. ⓐ Hovedgaden 16, Femmøller Strand
① 86 36 22 00 Ⓦ www.molskroen.dk

The Djursland coastline: cross country to Grenå

If you prefer to take in some inland adventures, there is plenty to see and do if you travel from east Djursland through some of the smaller towns and villages towards the seaside town of Grenå, the final stop on our coastal journey and Djursland's largest town. In this area you will also find three adjoining forests, Auning Skov, Fjeld Skov and Løvenholmskov.

⬇ *The Kattegatcentret is one of the biggest attractions in the area*

GETTING THERE

From Aarhus, the 60-km (37-mile) journey to Grenå takes
around 45 minutes, but the inland route will take you longer,
depending on how many of the sights you decide to take in.
Follow route 15 out of Aarhus (along Kystvejen and Skovvejen,
past Riis Skov) to go straight to Grenå. If you want to see some
inland sights, turn off heading east on route 587 just after you
pass Løgten. At the first major right, head north on route 563.
This will take you to the heart of Auning and on to route 16,
which ends up by the sea at Grenå.

⬤ The Hawaii installation at Djurs Sommerland

If you wish to take public transport, there are hourly trains from Århus H (see page 49) to Grenå.

SIGHTS & ATTRACTIONS

Allingåbro

Just 30 minutes' drive north of Aarhus is the small town of Allingåbro. Fans of motor vehicles should visit in May for the one-day **Allingåbro Motor Festival** (ⓐ Hovedgaden 27, Allingåbro ❶ 23 72 97 03 ⓦ www.motor-festival.dk Ⓝ Regional bus: 119 from

---

DJURS SOMMERLAND – DENMARK'S BIGGEST WATER PARK

Heading east along route 16, this is a superb place in which to shiver one's timbers and amuse one's children. As well as the fantastic waterslide, the Colorado River ride and Cowboyland, there are lovely gardens to relax in. There is a large picnic area with barbecues where you can prepare your own food, and several eateries selling healthy sandwiches and salads as well as fast food. The theme of the park is becoming distinctly more piratical, which, of course, the little ones just love as it may ring certain bells in their minds. Idea for a film: Pirates of the Jutland Peninsula. ⓐ Randersvej 17 ❶ 86 39 84 00 ⓦ www.djurssommerland.dk ❶ Irregular opening hours, check website for details Ⓝ Regional bus: 121 from Århus Rutebilstation ❶ Admission charge

Århus Rutebilstation), which brings together motorbike, car, truck, motocross and tractor enthusiasts from around Denmark. Some of the events include drag racing, stock car racing, a classic car exhibition and a freight trucker exhibition.

Djursland for fuld Damp (Full Steam Ahead in Djursland ⓐ Hovedgaden 4, Allingåbro ❶ 86 48 04 44 ⓦ www.dffd.dk ⓛ 09.00–17.00 daily (May–Sept) ⓝ Regional bus: 119 from Århus Rutebilstation) offers a variety of different activities including rental of a cycle-trolley. The tracks run through forests, fields and by the fjord with picnic areas to stop at along the way. There are also canoes to rent if you feel like a water adventure. In July and August, take a slow ride through the forest and along the fjord on an old steam train. You can also visit the small museum, hire an old bus for a sightseeing tour, or spend a few nights in an old sleeping car or in the old station warehouse, both of which have been converted to provide accommodation.

Auning Kart Park

Just to the south of Allingåbro is Auning. Denmark's best go-kart track, Auning Kart Park, is located halfway between the two. There are good facilities and a café and big terrace with a great view over the track for spectators. ⓐ Dammelstrupvej 1 ❶ 30 58 12 34 ⓦ www.auningkartpark.dk ⓛ Hours vary (Mar–Nov), check website for details; by appointment (Nov–Mar) ⓝ Regional bus: 119 from Århus Rutebilstation ❶ Admission charge, under 18s free

Djurslands Jernbanemuseum (Djursland Railway Museum)

Just south of Djurs Sommerland in the town of Ryomgård, you'll find this tiny museum where you can visit the train depot which dates back to 1908, see the exhibition telling the history of Danish railways, take a look at some of the old steam-train engines and carriages, or admire the wonderfully detailed model railways. ⓐ Museumsvej 2 ⓣ 86 39 59 11 ⓦ www.djbm.dk ⓛ Hours vary, check website for details ⓝ Regional bus: 121 from Århus Rutebilstation; Århus H–Grenå train to Ryomgård ⓘ Admission charge

Grenå

Historically a market town, Grenå has several different types of specialist shops and supermarkets and a fairly busy harbour. Grenå Å (Grenå River) runs through the town centre, linking it to the harbour. At the heart of the town is Torvet (the Square) with the church at its centre. Just opposite the church you'll find the tourist information **Grenå Turistbureau** (ⓐ Torvet 1 ⓣ 87 58 12 00 ⓦ www.visitdjursland.com). The long, sandy, white Grenå Strand is one of Jutland's best beaches, due to its child-friendliness, excellent facilities and extremely clean water.

Probably the most famous tourist attraction in Grenå is **Kattegatcentret (Kattegat Centre** ⓐ Færgevej 4 ⓣ 86 32 52 00 ⓦ www.kattegatcentret.dk ⓛ Hours vary considerably during the year, check website or call for details). This amazing marine wildlife centre is one of a kind where both adults and children have the opportunity to get into closer contact with marine life. The centre has created a spacious environment for its inhabitants and visitors. The massive aquariums allow you to get a close view of hundreds of different types of marine life. There is daily feeding of the sharks, seals and the fish in the

● *View all the marine life while 'in the water' at the Kattegatcentret*

tropical lagoon, and you can do an introductory scuba dive in the same tanks as the sharks.

Skandinavisk Dyrepark (Scandinavian Wildlife Park)

Great for nature lovers, this fantastic park in Kolind is set in authentic Scandinavian countryside and is home to over 300 animals. From brown bears to landrace goats, moose and wolves, the animals have plenty of space to roam around in their natural environment. The Mammoth Activity Centre is the only place in Europe where you can see a full-sized mammoth skeleton.

ⓐ Nødagervej 67B ⓣ 86 39 13 33 ⓦ www.skandinaviskdyrepark.dk
🕙 10.00–17.00 daily (May, June & mid-Aug–Sept); 10.00–18.00

daily (July–mid-Aug); 10.00–16.00 Tues–Thur, 10.00–17.00 Sat & Sun, closed Mon & Fri (Sept–mid-Oct); 10.00–17.00 daily (annual autumn holiday only, call to check dates) ⓝ Regional bus: 120 from Århus Rutebilstation; Århus H–Grenå train to Kolind ⓘ Admission charge

CULTURE

Djurslands Museum & Dansk Fiskerimuseum (Djursland Museum & Danish Fishing Museum)

These are housed in the beautiful old half-timbered yellow building near the church on the main square of Grenå. Together, the museums have a curious collection of artefacts dating back to the year 1000. ⓐ Søndergade 1, Grenå ⓣ 86 32 48 00 ⓦ www.djurslandsmuseum.dk ⓛ 11.00–16.00 Mon–Fri, 12.00–15.00 Sat & Sun (July & Aug); 13.00–16.00 Tues–Fri, 12.00–15.00 Sun, closed Mon & Sat (Sept–June)

Gammel Estrup & Dansk Landbrugsmuseum

Close to the town of Auning, you will find two wonderful places of historical interest. The first is Gammel Estrup, a museum housed in the beautiful Gammel Estrup Manor House, whose farmhouses are home to the second attraction, Dansk Landbrugsmuseum (Danish Agricultural Museum).

Gammel Estrup is a beautiful Renaissance manor with a Baroque garden and carp ponds. Through changing exhibitions and events visitors to the museum can learn about the life of the Danish aristocracy (and their servants). As well as the permanent exhibition, there are activities happening all year round in which staff dress in period costume. ⓐ Randersvej 2, Auning ⓣ 86 48 30 01 ⓦ www.gammelestrup.dk ⓛ Hours vary, check website for details

The Dansk Landbrugsmuseum is an agricultural museum. Its huge collection of old vehicles and farming equipment brings you close to some of the past wonders of the farming world. The old smithy is housed in a building that dates back to 1761. ⓐ Randersvej 4, Auning ⓣ 86 48 34 44 ⓦ www.gl-estrup.dk ⓛ 10.00–15.00 Tues–Sun, closed Mon (Feb, Mar, Nov & Dec);

⬧ The Djurslands Museum & Dansk Fiskerimuseum in the centre of Grenå

10.00–17.00 daily (Apr–June & mid-Aug–Oct); 10.00–18.00 daily (July–mid-Aug)

RETAIL THERAPY

All of the aforementioned sights, attractions and cultural institutes have their own gift shops where you can purchase souvenirs of your trip. If you are a pottery lover, you should visit **Pottehuset**, north of Nimtofte in Nørager, to find high-quality Danish pottery. ⓐ Keramikvej 6 ⓣ 86 48 63 65 ⓦ www.pottehuset.net ⓛ 10.00–17.00 daily (Whitsun–mid-Sept)

TAKING A BREAK

If the weather is fine, you really should take advantage of the marvellous countryside and bring along a picnic hamper. Alternatively, grab a bite to eat at the eateries found in the larger attractions listed. There are a few different places to try in the larger town, Grenå, but do not expect to find many food options in the smaller towns and villages.

AFTER DARK

There is not much to do in these locations after dark, so your best bet is to either head back to Aarhus or down to Ebeltoft (see page 112).

Helnan Marina Hotel ££ This hotel in Grenå has a lovely restaurant with an exciting, international menu that's designed according

⬤ *The wild landscape of the coastline near Gjerrild, north of Grenå*

to what is in season. ⓐ Kystvej 32, Grenå ⓣ 86 32 25 00
🕐 18.00–22.00 Mon–Sat, closed Sun

ACCOMMODATION

For cheaper options, head to Danhostel Rønde or Ebeltoft
(see page 112). Otherwise in Grenå there are the Helnan Marina
Hotel (see above) or the nearby **Gjerrild Kro**, a wonderful
Danish inn with nineteen rooms in two buildings that date
back to 1843. ⓐ Gjerrild Bygade 16, Gjerrild ⓣ 86 38 40 51
ⓦ www.gjerrild-kro.dk

▶ *Find your way to Aarhus by air, rail, road or ferry*

PRACTICAL
information

Directory

GETTING THERE

By air

Ryanair is the only budget airline currently operating flights from London Stansted to Aarhus Airport (see page 48). In addition, from Aarhus Airport Scandinavian Airlines operates scheduled flights to and from Copenhagen, British Airways to and from Oslo, Gothenburg and Stockholm. From Billund Lufthavn, which has a one-hour bus connection to Aarhus, there are scheduled flights to all the major cities in Europe, such as Amsterdam, Berlin, Prague, London, Gothenburg, Madrid, Milan, Munich and Dublin. In England there are connections to Billund via British Airways to and from London and Manchester, Cimber Sterling to and from London Gatwick and Ryanair to and from London Stansted.

British Airways Ⓦ www.ba.com
Cimber Sterling Ⓦ www.cimber.com
Ryanair Ⓦ www.ryanair.com
Scandinavian Airlines (SAS) Ⓦ www.sas.dk

Many people are aware that air travel emits CO_2, which contributes to climate change. You may be interested in the possibility of lessening the environmental impact of your flight through the charity **Climate Care**, which offsets your CO_2 by funding environmental projects around the world. Visit Ⓦ www.jpmorganclimatecare.com

By rail

This is probably the most expensive way to arrive in Aarhus unless you are travelling on an **Interrail**, **Eurorail** or **Scanrail** ticket (Ⓦ www.scanrail.com). At **Rail Europe** (Ⓦ www.raileurope.co.uk), you can book tickets online. A journey from the UK by rail will first involve a ferry journey from Harwich to Esbjerg in Jutland (see page 129) or the **Eurostar** train from London to Brussels (Ⓘ (UK) 08705 186186 Ⓦ www.eurostar.com). Århus H is the main train station in the city (see page 49).

By road

It is great to have a car if you are planning a longer stay as Aarhus is surrounded by beautiful countryside, and the rest of Jutland

🔺 *Yellow city buses and blue regional buses pass the Rådhus*

offers numerous holidaying possibilities. Arriving from the UK, the least complicated route is to take the ferry from Harwich to Esbjerg (see opposite). From Zealand, take either one of the ferry options, or from Korsø drive across the Strobæltsbroen bridge and another of Denmark's islands, Fyn. This will take you to Jutland, which is 75 minutes south of Aarhus. If you are already on mainland Europe, the easiest route is through Germany via Hamburg (Jutland connects to Germany's northern border). For detailed road directions see ⓦ www.bing.com/maps

Coach options are underwhelming. **Eurolines Scandinavia** offers a very limited service to Aarhus but does not have an office in the city (ⓣ 33 88 70 00 ⓦ www.eurolines.dk). There is a coach (No 888) that operates between Copenhagen and Aalborg, stopping in Aarhus at the main bus station, **Rutebilstation**

⬢ *Aarhus's busy harbour*

(ⓐ Fredensgade & Copenhagen Airport (Valby S-train station in the city – see ⓦ www.dsb.dk for further connections in Copenhagen)). The journey takes around three hours, and there are up to six departures a day. ⓐ Graham Bellsvej 40 ⓣ 70 21 08 88 ⓦ www.abildskou.dk

By water

Coming from England you can take the ferry from Harwich to Esbjerg. **DFDS Seaways** has three scheduled departures per week all year round (ⓣ (UK) 0871 522 9955 (DK) 33 423 000 ⓦ www.dfds.co.uk). The trip from Esbjerg to Aarhus will take just under two hours by road or by train.

Travelling to and from Zealand, where Copenhagen is located, **Mols Linien** (ⓣ 70 10 14 18 ⓦ www.mols-linien.dk) operates two routes: Aarhus to Odden (45-minute boat trip; 90 minutes to Copenhagen) and Aarhus to Kalundborg (65-minute boat trip; 75 minutes to Copenhagen). There is no public transport from either port on Zealand, so a car is a must.

ENTRY FORMALITIES

If you have an EU, US, Canadian, Australian or New Zealand passport, you do not need a visa; all other nationalities will require one. However, for stays longer than three months a residence permit is required. EU citizens can apply for this while in Denmark, but other nationals must obtain one before entering the country. Immigration control is very tight and you will be questioned about where you are staying, the purpose of your visit and how you intend to support yourself. EU residents may bring possessions and goods for personal use (including tobacco

and alcohol) into Denmark, provided they have been bought
in the EU. Residents of non-EU countries, and EU residents
arriving from a non-EU country, are limited to a maximum of:
400 cigarettes and 50 cigars or 50 g (2 oz) tobacco; two litres
(three bottles) of wine and one litre (approximately two pints)
of spirits or liqueurs.

MONEY

The currency in Denmark is the Danish krone (kr) and the smaller
units are øre (100øre = 1kr). Øre come in 25 and 50 øre pieces and
are bronze in colour. The 1, 2 and 5kr pieces are silver in colour and
ascend in size as with value. The 10 and 20kr pieces are golden
colour, the 10kr being smaller in size than the 20kr. The main place
to change money in Aarhus is at the banks which are located on
the main streets in the city. Look out for Nordea, Jyske Bank, Spar
Nord and Djurslands Bank. Banks do not keep large amounts of
foreign currency, so make sure you change some at home. Forex
bureau de change found on the main shopping street will have
larger sums at hand (ⓐ Ryesgade 28 ⓣ 86 80 03 40). Where there
are banks, there are ATMs. Visa and MasterCard are accepted in
most of the larger stores, but many of the smaller ones might not
accept foreign (non-Danish) credit cards.

HEALTH, SAFETY & CRIME

No vaccinations or preventative medicines need to be taken
before arriving in Denmark. The water is very clean and safe
to drink from the tap. The Danish healthcare system is good.
EU citizens need to have their European Health Insurance Card
(EHIC) in order to claim any healthcare expenses upon return to

their home country. A doctor's consultation will cost a minimum of 300kr. Travel insurance is essential to ensure you are covered in any case.

Aarhus is probably one of the safest cities in northern Europe. The most trouble you may run into is when the nightclubs turn out in the early hours of the morning and there may be a few exuberant merrymakers roaming the streets around Vadestedet. Even so, do not take any unnecessary risks. If you do have anything stolen, report it immediately to the police so that you can claim it on your insurance (see Emergencies, page 136, for numbers).

OPENING HOURS

Shops usually open at 09.30 or 10.00 and close 17.30 Monday to Thursday, 18.00–19.00 Friday and 14.00–15.00 Saturday. The bigger stores may have longer opening hours on Friday and Saturday. Shops are closed on Sunday. Many museums and attractions have late opening on Wednesday (until 20.00–21.00) and are closed on Sunday. Some of the smaller ones also close on Monday. Restaurants open at widely varying times, some from as early as 10.00, but most close their kitchen between 21.30 and 22.00. Banks are open 10.00–16.00 Monday to Friday and some open until 17.30 on Thursday.

TOILETS

There are public toilets in the main train and bus station. The department stores and some larger shops also have toilets. Staff at restaurants, bars and cafés don't usually mind if you ask to use theirs. There are also several modern public toilets throughout the city – they look like big, grey Tardises.

CHILDREN

Aarhus is very child-friendly, as is the rest of Denmark. Entrance to most of the museums is free for under 18s. Local buses and all trains accommodate pushchairs and prams; public buildings have lifts and ramps and people at hand to help. People offer to help if they can see you need it.

Most of the museums and attractions have a children's section. The junior museum in ARoS (see page 66) is a particular favourite and the Barndommens Museum in the Kvindemuseet (see page 69) is extremely popular as it is a celebration of childhood. As well as Tivoli Friheden (see page 95) there is **Legeland** (ⓐ Holmstrupgårdvej 18, Braband

● *Viking imagery on show at ARoS*

86 24 11 22 **www.legelandet.dk** **10.00–18.00 Thur–Sun,**
closed Mon–Wed (open daily in school holidays) Bus: 15 to
Holmstrupgårdvej Admission charge), located just outside the
city centre. This is a huge indoor playground with massive slides,
bouncy castles and mini-golf. Just south of the city you will find
Moesgård Museum (see page 94), an open-air museum with a
forest and the beach as its boundaries, which is a great place to
take children. This archaeological and ethnographical museum
has numerous activities for children and is a fun, educational
day out for the whole family.

COMMUNICATIONS
Internet
Internet cafés are non-existent in the city centre as everybody
has access at home in Denmark. However, many cafés and
public offices have free wireless access, as do the majority of
hotels. The hostels, sleep-ins and several bed & breakfasts have
Internet access. You can use the computers in public libraries
for free.

Phone
There are a few public telephones around, and they are either
card- or coin-operated. Phonecards come in denominations of
30, 50 and 100kr, and the coin-operated phones accept all coins
from 1 to 20kr but do not give change.

If you are using your home mobile phone to call a Danish
number, don't forget to precede the number with the country
code for Denmark (45). So if you have an English phone then
you would dial 0045 plus the eight-digit Danish number.

TELEPHONING DENMARK

The international dialling code for Denmark is 45. To dial any of the Danish numbers in this book from your own country, dial your own international access code (oo for the UK), then 45, then the eight-digit number. All private phones in Denmark have eight digits and there are no area codes.

TELEPHONING ABROAD

To dial abroad from Denmark, dial oo followed by your own country's international code (UK 44, Ireland 353, USA and Canada 1, Australia 61, New Zealand 64, South Africa 27) and then the area code (leaving off the first o) and number.

Post

Letters weighing up to 50 g to destinations within Denmark are 5.50kr. The same letter will cost 8.50kr to a European destination and 9kr to the rest of the world.

Main Post Office ⓐ Banegårdspladsen 1A ❶ 80 20 70 30 ⓦ www.postdanmark.dk ⓛ 10.00–18.00 Mon–Fri, 10.00–13.00 Sat, closed Sun

ELECTRICITY

Denmark runs on 220V 50Hz AC and the Danish sockets are round two-pin ones. Adaptors are best bought in your home country, but you can find multi-pin adaptors in some electrical stores. Hotels will have square adaptors you can borrow.

TRAVELLERS WITH DISABILITIES

Aarhus is an extremely socially aware city, therefore you will find that almost all public areas, toilets and buildings, including shops and restaurants, are accessible to the disabled. Bus and train drivers are happy to help passengers embark and alight. For further information contact **Socialcenter Centrum** (ⓐ Valdemarsgade 18 ⓣ 89 40 20 00).

TOURIST INFORMATION

VisitAarhus Velkomstcenter is located near the main train station (ⓐ Banegårdspladsen 20 ⓣ 87 31 50 10 ⓦ www.visitaarhus.com ⓗ Hours vary from year to year and from season to season, check website for details ⓥ Bus: all routes to Banegårdspladsen).

BACKGROUND READING

Most of the books about Aarhus are only in Danish and have no English translation. However, the following will give you excellent background information on some of the key influences on the city:

Danish Chairs by Noritsugu Oda. This highly readable work provides explanation and context for the national obsession with design.

No Small Achievement: Special Operations Executive and the Danish Resistance, 1940–1945 by Knud J V Jespersen and Christopher Wade. A fascinating account of how the Danish psyche dealt with five years of occupation.

The Vikings by Else Roesdahl. The best of the many books about the horny-helmeted marauders who gave Aarhus its start in life.

Emergencies

For emergency fire, ambulance & police call ☎ 112 (toll-free)

MEDICAL SERVICES
Your hotel will have a list of doctors in the area. The fee must be paid in cash and will be a minimum of 300kr. Almost all doctors will speak excellent English.

Emergency medical professionals
Emergency doctor ☎ 70 11 31 31 ⏰ 16.00–08.00 Mon–Fri, 24 hours Sat & Sun
Emergency dentist ☎ 40 11 89 90 Mon–Fri, 40 51 51 62 Sat & Sun
Emergency chiropractor ☎ 86 18 00 00
24-hour pharmacy – Løve Apotek ⓐ Store Torv 5 ☎ 86 12 00 22

EMERGENCY PHRASES

Help! Can you help me?
Hjælp! Kan du hjæpe mig?
Yehlb! Ka do yehlbeh mai?

Call an ambulance/a doctor/the police!
Ring efter en ambulance/en læge/politiet!
Ring ehfda in ahmboolahnseh/in leh-eh/porlitee-eht!

Accident & Emergency – Århus Sygehus 🅰 Nørrebrogade 44
☎ 89 49 44 44 🆆 www.aarhussygehus.dk Ⓝ Bus: 14, 56, 58 to
Århus Sygehus

POLICE

If you break down in your car, call **Falck** (☎ 70 10 20 30).

Should you need to report a crime or a theft, contact
Århus Police (🅰 Riddestræde 1 ☎ 87 31 14 48 Ⓝ Bus: 3, 7, 14
to Rutebilstation).

EMBASSIES & CONSULATES

All embassies and consulates are located in Copenhagen.
You should contact the embassy if you need a replacement
passport. For matters involving the police, the embassy will
be unable to assist you.

Australian 🅰 Dampfærgevej 26 ☎ 70 26 36 76
🆆 www.denmark.embassy.gov.au
British 🅰 Kastelsvej 36–40 ☎ 35 44 52 00
🆆 www.ukindenmark.fco.gov.uk
Canadian 🅰 Kristen Bernikowsgade 1 ☎ 33 48 32 00
🆆 www.canadainternational.gc.ca
Irish 🅰 Østbanegade 21 ☎ 35 42 32 33 ✉ irlemb@e-mail.dk
South African 🅰 Gammel Vartov Vej 8 ☎ 39 18 01 55
🆆 www.southafrica.dk
US 🅰 Dag Hammarskjölds Allé 24 ☎ 35 41 71 00
🆆 www.denmark.usembassy.gov

ACKNOWLEDGEMENTS

The publishers would like to thank the following individuals and organisations for supplying their copyright photographs for this book: Alamy (Alan Spencer), page 125; Århus Festuge/Wikimedia Commons, page 9; Arne Bramsen/ BigStockPhoto.com, page 124; Nicol Foulkes, pages 33, 96 & 127; Steffen Højager/Dreamstime.com, page 57; Pieter Kuiper/Wikimedia Commons, page 116; Rasmus Laursen/ Wikimedia Commons, page 47; Lorna/Dreamstime.com, page 101; Antony Mcaulay/Dreamstime.com, page 5; Mikkel Østergaard/ Dreamstime.com, page 82; Photoshot, page 23; Jean Schweitze/ Dreamstime.com, page 122; Visit Denmark, all others

Project editor: Karen Beaulah
Copy editor: Paul Hines
Layout: Trevor Double
Proofreaders: Cath Senker & Karolin Thomas

Send your thoughts to
books@thomascook.com

- **Found a great bar, club, shop or must-see sight that we don't feature?**

- **Like to tip us off about any information that needs a little updating?**

- **Want to tell us what you love about this handy little guidebook and more importantly how we can make it even handier?**

Then here's your chance to tell all! Send us ideas, discoveries and recommendations today and then look out for your valuable input in the next edition of this title.

Email the above address (stating the title) or write to: pocket guides Series Editor, Thomas Cook Publishing, PO Box 227, Coningsby Road, Peterborough PE3 8SB, UK.

Useful phrases

English	Danish	*Approx pronunciation*
BASICS		
Yes	Ja	*Ya*
No	Nej	*Nai*
Thank you	Tak	*Tahg*
Hello	Hej	*Hai*
Goodbye	Hej hej	*Hai hai*
Excuse me	Undskyld	*Ornskewl*
Sorry	Undskyld	*Ornskewl*
That's okay	Det er i orden	*Di air ee orrdehn*
To	Til	*Ti*
From	Fra	*Frah*
Do you speak English?	Taler du engelsk?	*Tala do ehng-ehlsg?*
Good morning	Godmorgen	*Gor-morn*
Good afternoon	Goddag	*Gor-day*
Good evening	Godaften	*Gor-ahfdehn*
Goodnight	Godnat	*Goh-nad*
My name is ...	Mit navn er ...	*Mid nown air ...*
NUMBERS		
One	En	*In*
Two	To	*Tor*
Three	Tre	*Trreh*
Four	Fire	*Feerr*
Five	Fem	*Fem*
Six	Seks	*Sex*
Seven	Syv	*Suw*
Eight	Otte	*Ordeh*
Nine	Ni	*Nee*
Ten	Ti	*Tee*
Twenty	Tyve	*Toova*
Fifty	Halvtreds	*Haltrrehs*
One hundred	Hundrede	*Hoonner*
SIGNS & NOTICES		
Airport	Lufthavn	*Loofft-houn*
Rail station/Platform	Togstation/Perron	*Toe-stashion/Perr-on*
Smoking/ **Non-smoking**	Rygning/ Rygning forbudt	*Rooning/ Rooning forboot*
Toilets	Toiletter	*Toiledder*
Open/Closed	Åben/Lukket	*Orrban/Lorrk-ed*

WHAT'S IN YOUR GUIDEBOOK?

Independent authors Impartial up-to-date information from our travel experts who meticulously source local knowledge.

Experience Thomas Cook's 165 years in the travel industry and guidebook publishing enriches every word with expertise you can trust.

Travel know-how Thomas Cook has thousands of staff working around the globe, all living and breathing travel.

Editors Travel-publishing professionals, pulling everything together to craft a perfect blend of words, pictures, maps and design.

You, the traveller We deliver a practical, no-nonsense approach to information, geared to how you really use it.

ABOUT THE AUTHOR
Based in Copenhagen, Nicol Foulkes arrived in Denmark a decade ago, fell in love with the people and their lifestyle and decided to stay. Nicol works as a freelance travel writer, teacher, language consultant and cultural coach. She has studied and worked in England, Spain, Germany and Australia and has travelled extensively worldwide.